LETTER TRACING FOR TODDLERS

EMMA

TRACE MY NAME WORKBOOK

Can't Find Your Name?

Have our elves create a personalized book
with the name of your choice today!

VISIT US AT:
PERSONALIZETHISBOOK.COM

Cover and page design by Cool Journals Studios - Copyright 2017

ABOUT ME

MY NAME IS:

Emma

I LIVE IN:

For parents

For kids

I AM ☐ YEARS OLD.

DRAW YOU AND YOUR FAMILY

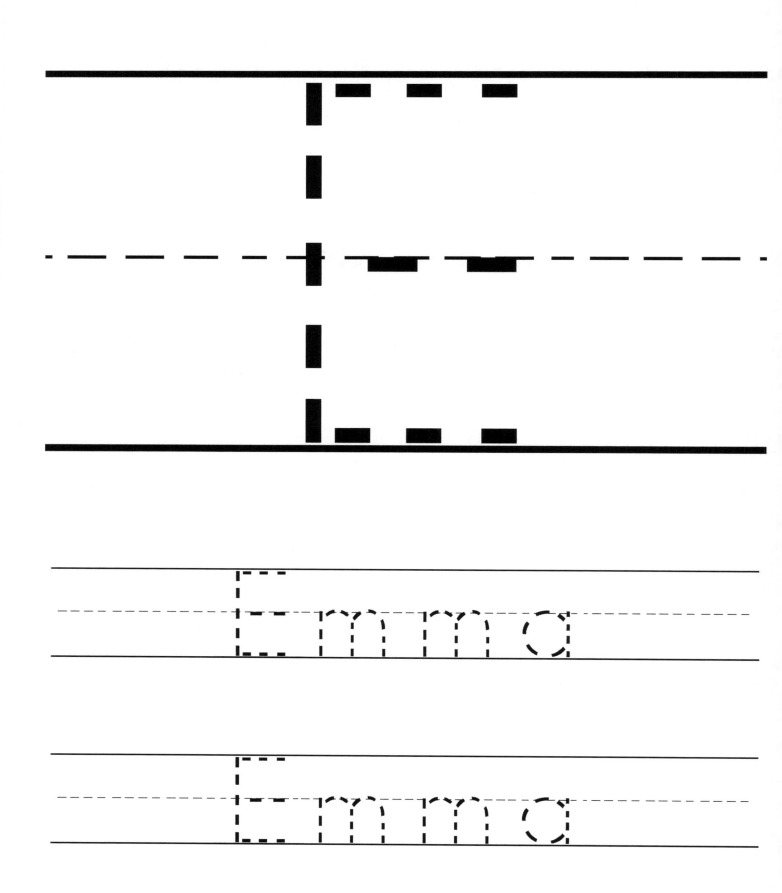

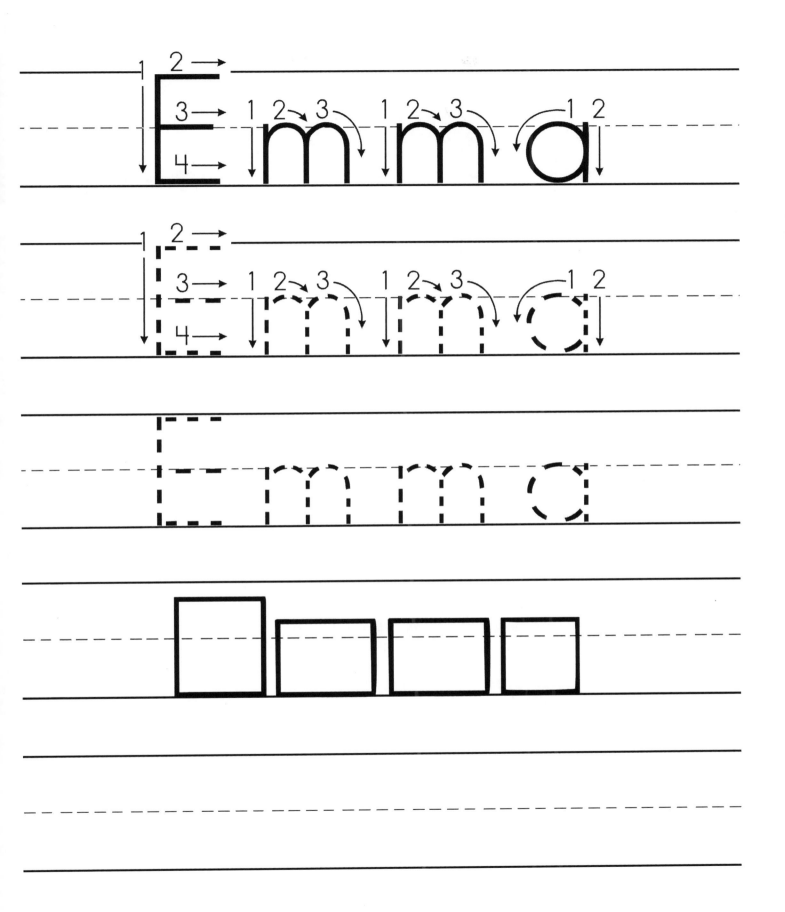

THIS IS HOW I WRITE MY NAME

MY NAME HAS ___ LETTERS

1	2	3	4	5	6	7	8

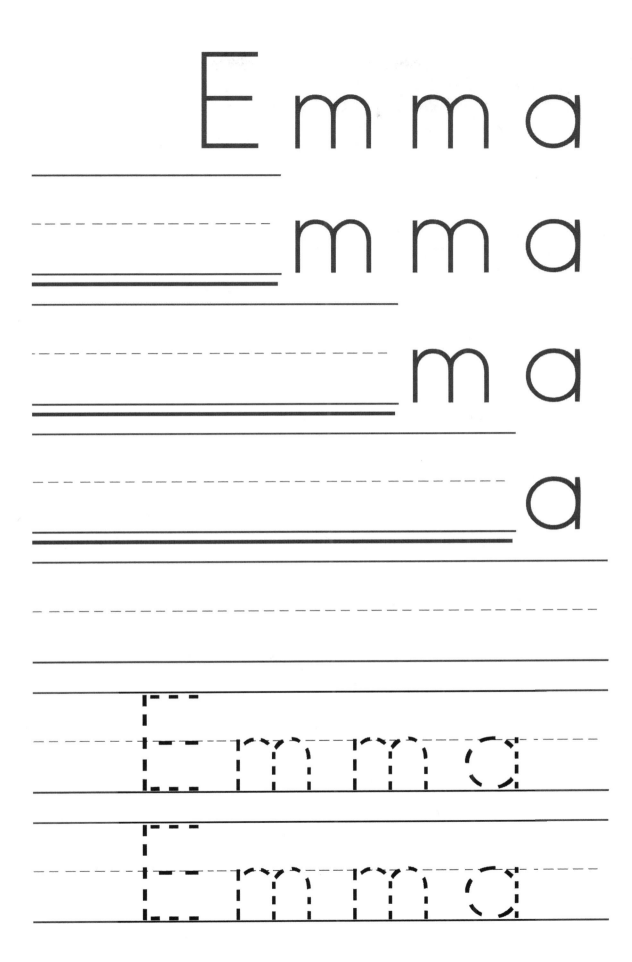

COLOR THE EGGS WITH LETTERS OF OUR NAME WRITE YOUR NAME

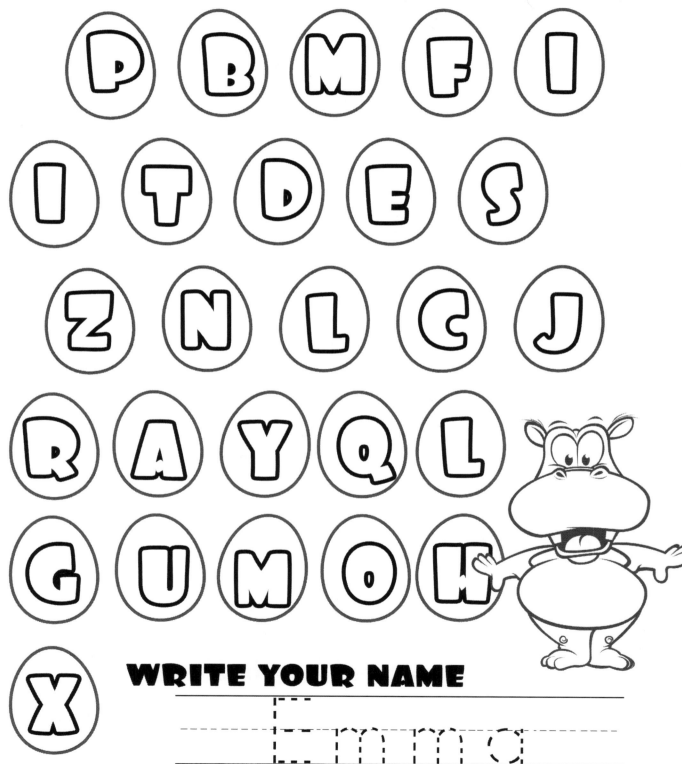

P B M F I
I T D E S
Z N L C J
R A Y Q L
G U M O K
X

WRITE YOUR NAME

Emma

WRITE YOU NAME WITH.

PEN

Emma

CRAYON

Emma

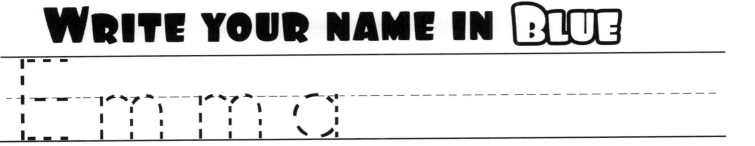

WRITE YOUR NAME IN BLUE

Emma

WRITE YOUR NAME IN YELLOW

Emma

DRAW YOUR FAVORITE THINGS

COLOR

FOOD

TOY

ANIMAL

MY NAME

My name starts with

_____

My name ends with

_____

FILL THE LETTERS OF YOUR NAME WHITH DIFFERENT COLORS

P B I F V I T
D E S L N L C
J R A Y Q K
G U M O H M

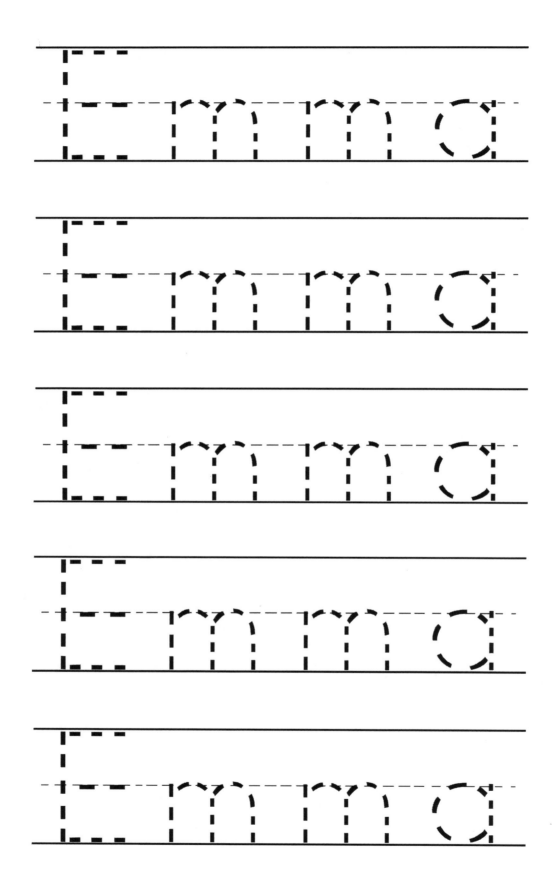

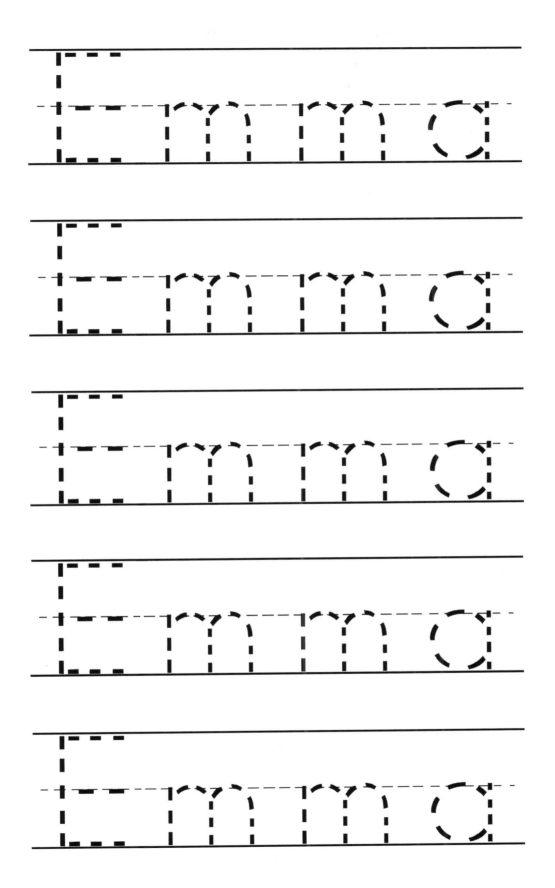

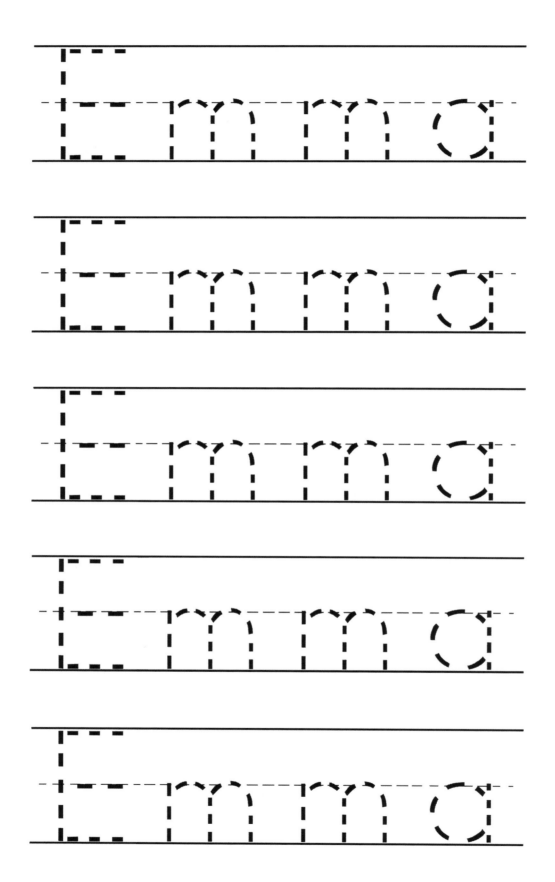

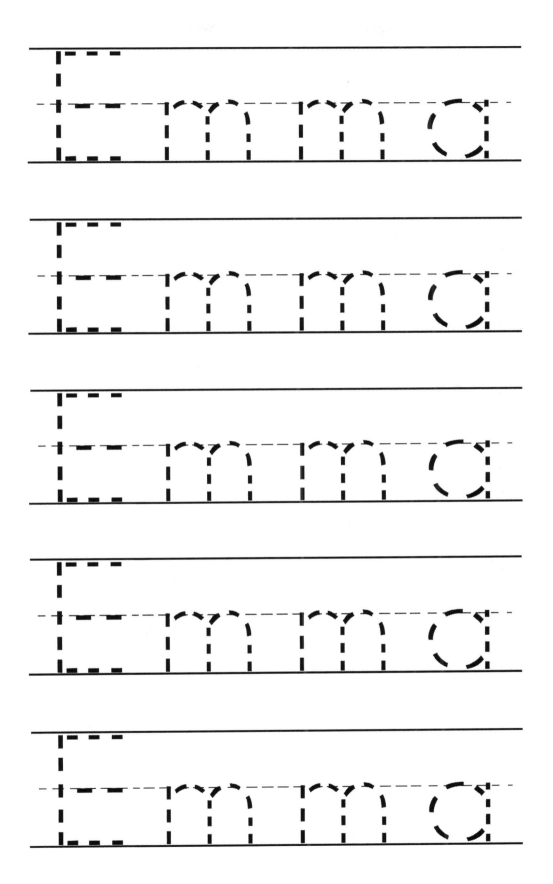

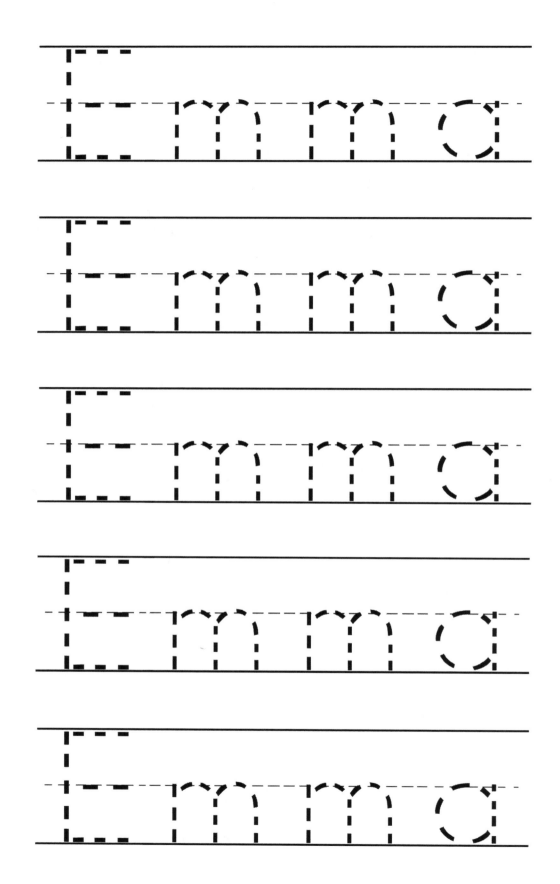

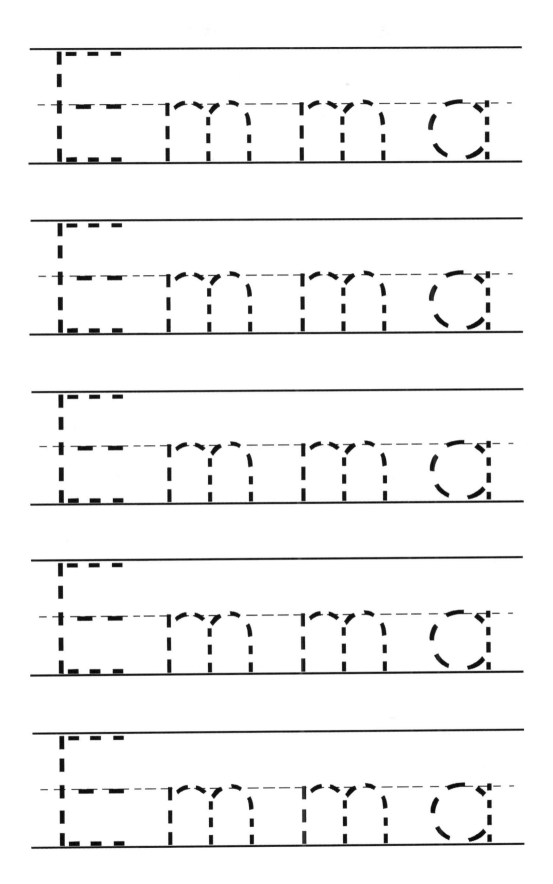

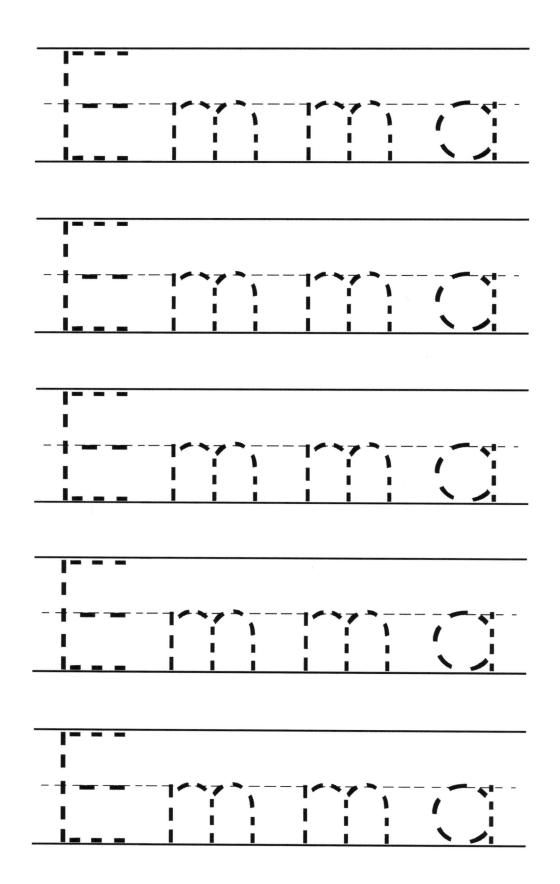

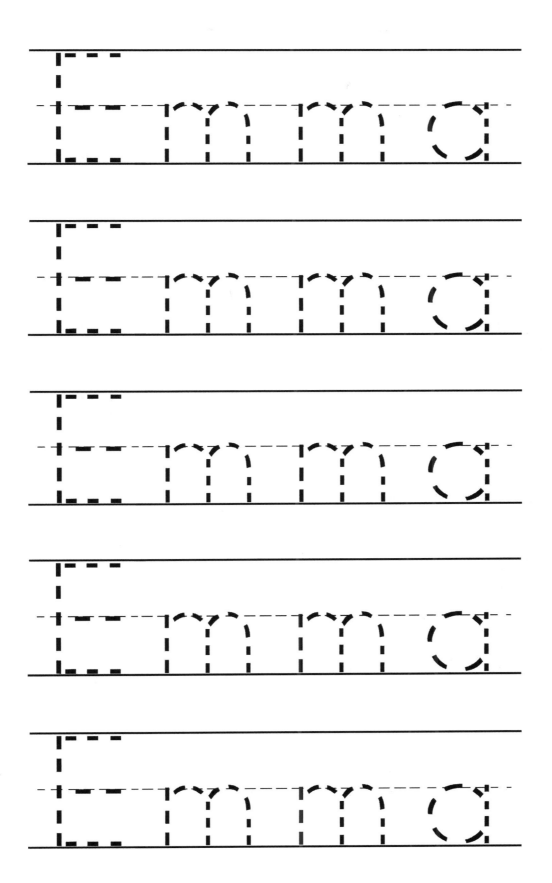

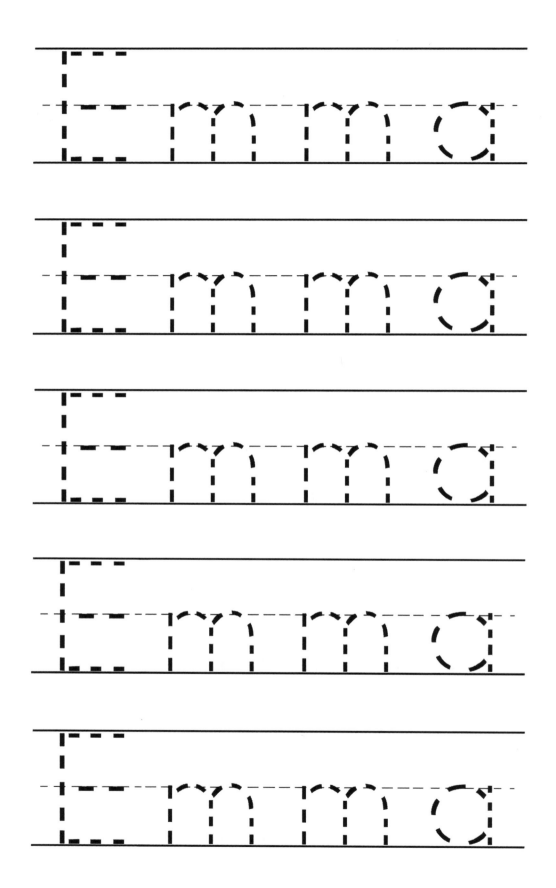

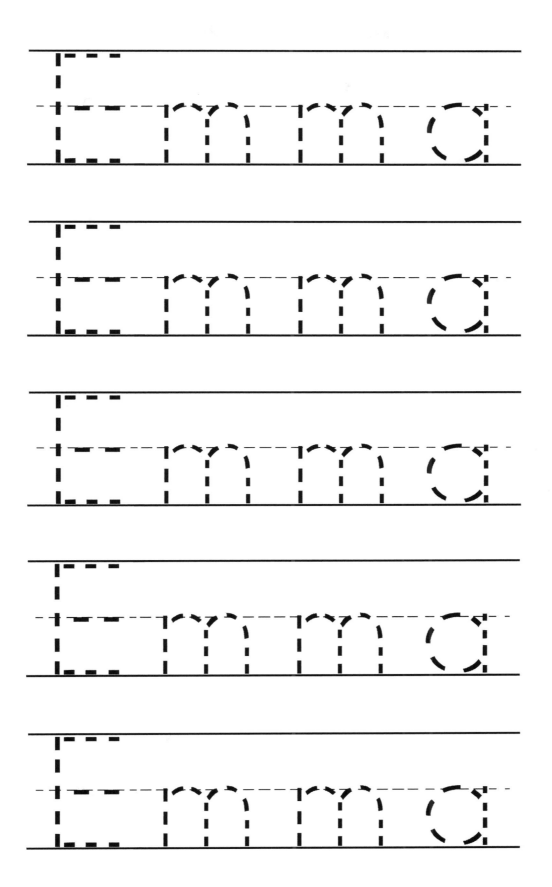

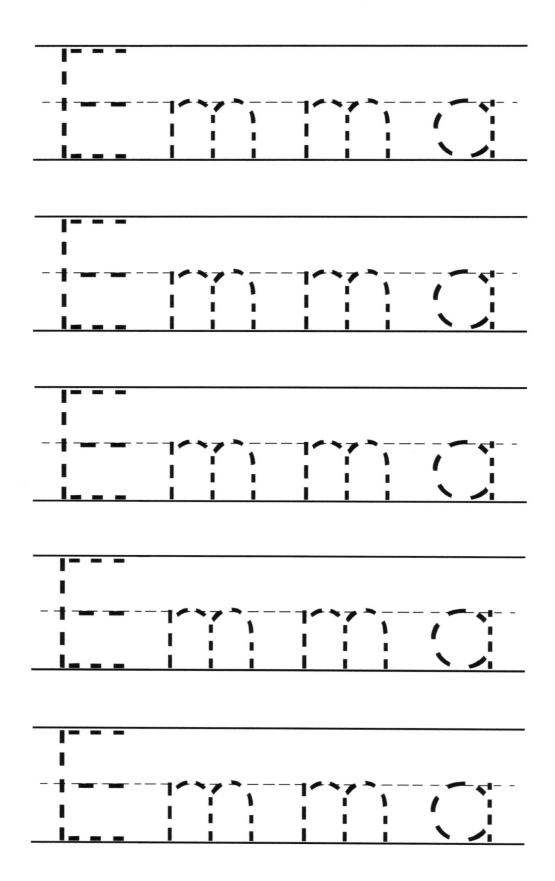

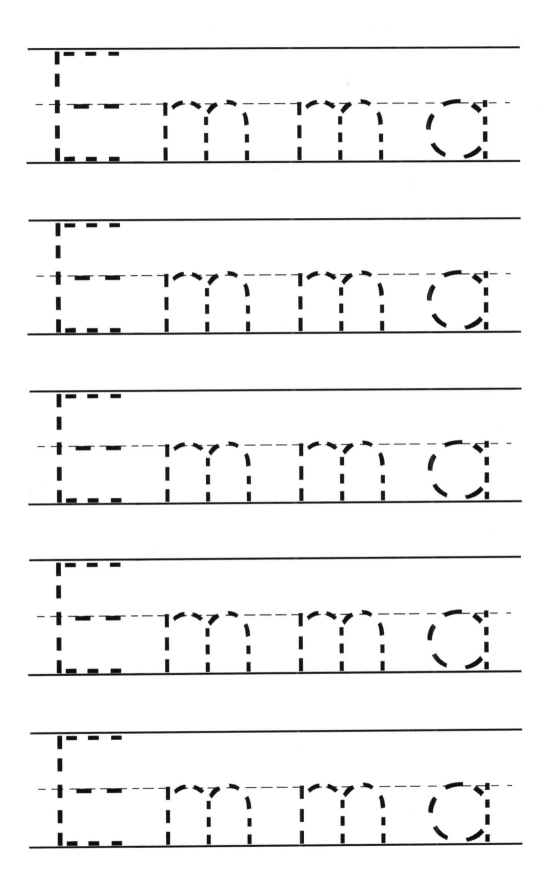

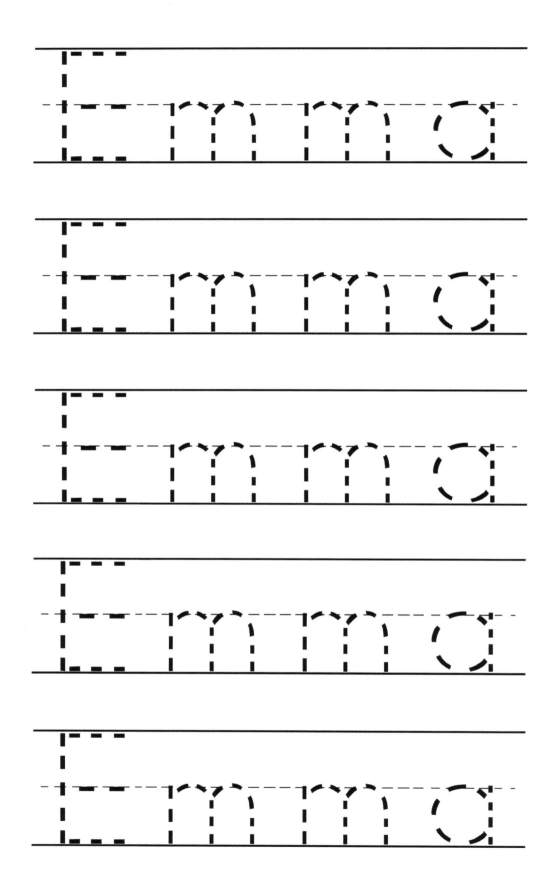

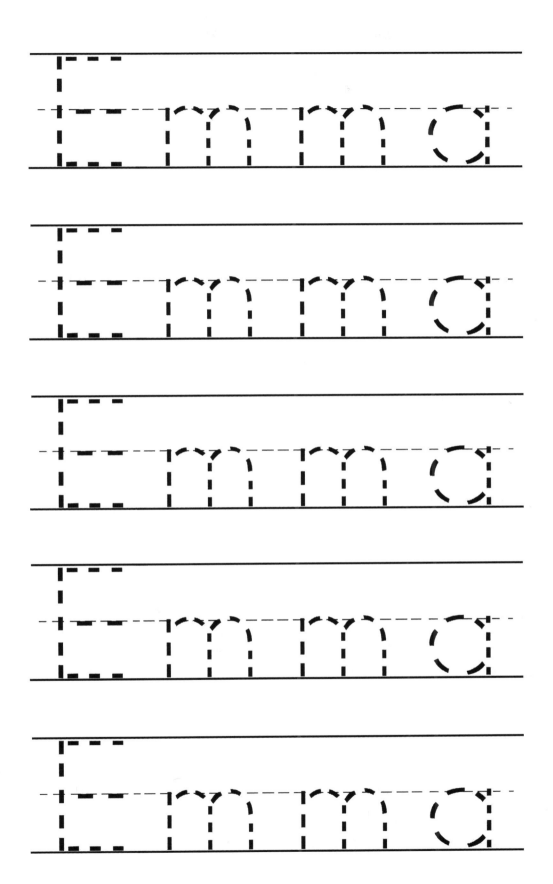

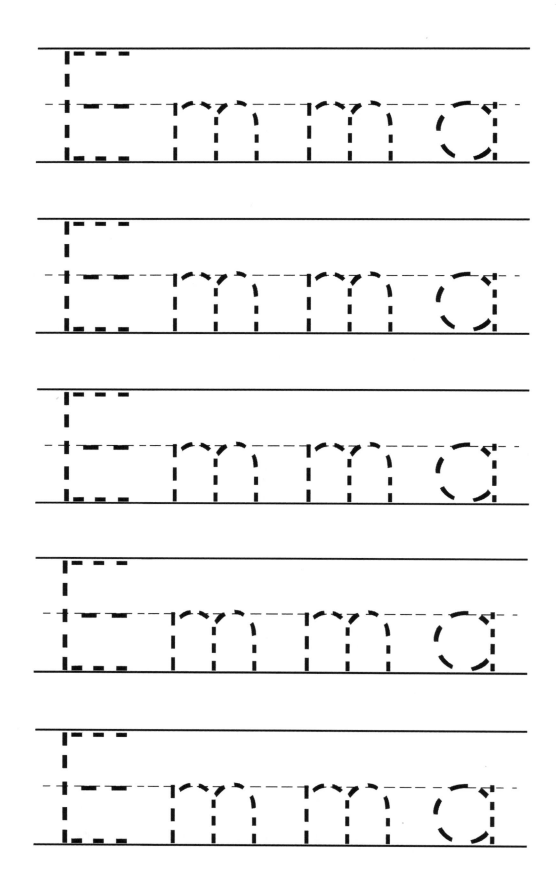

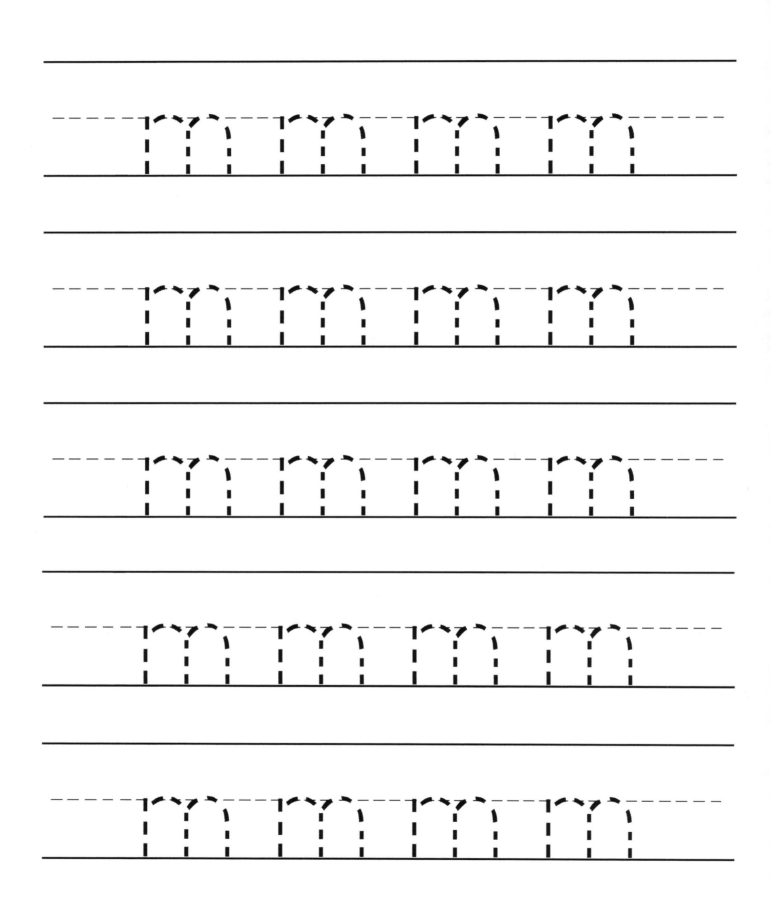

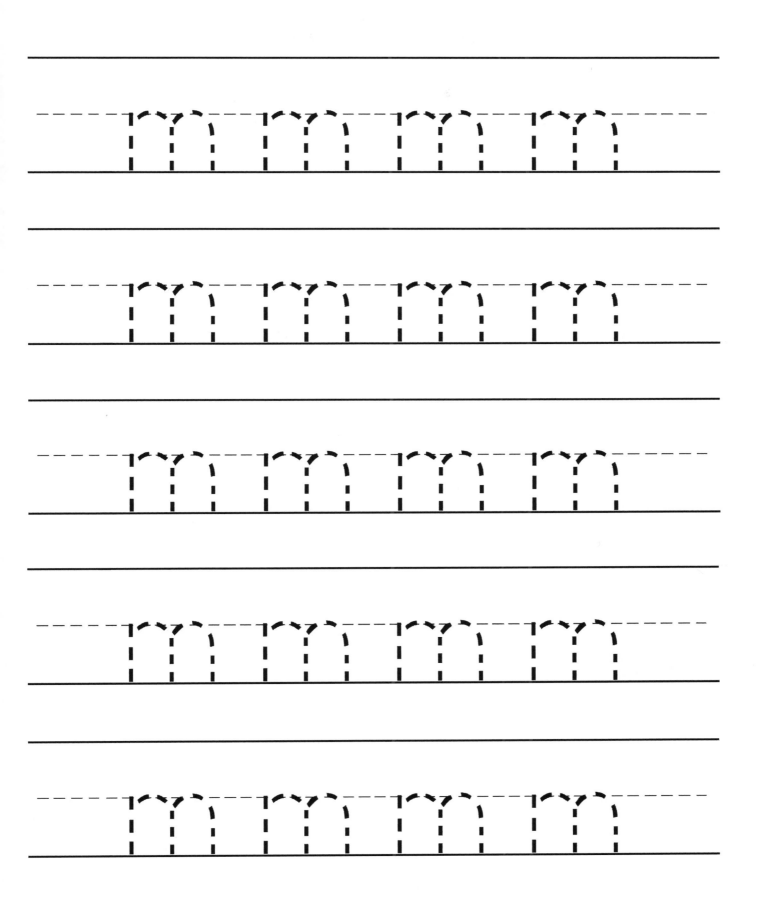

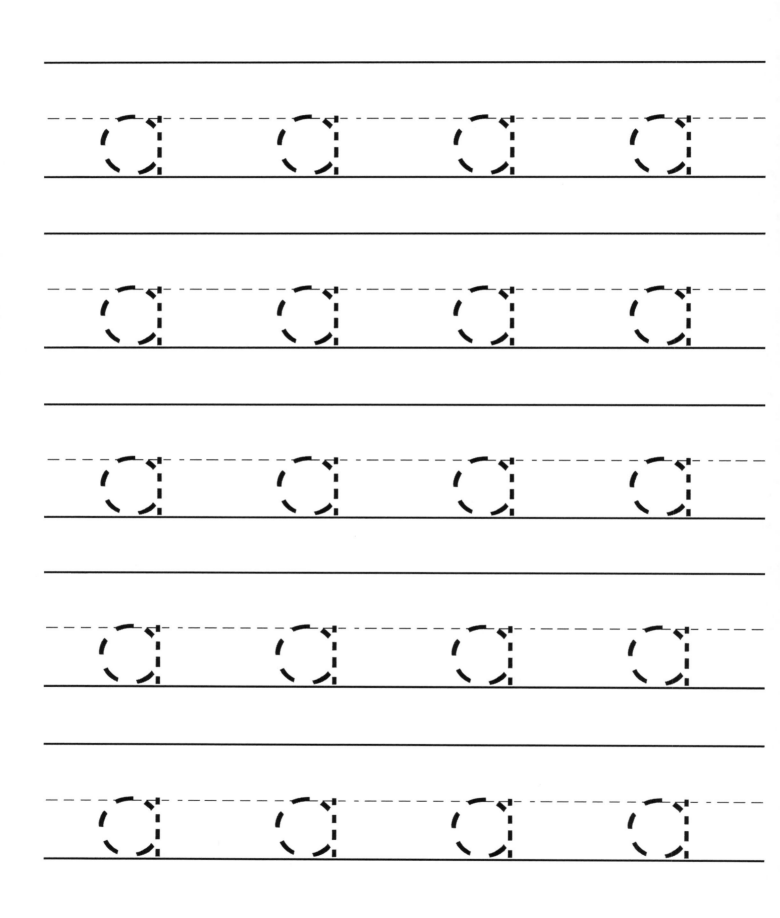

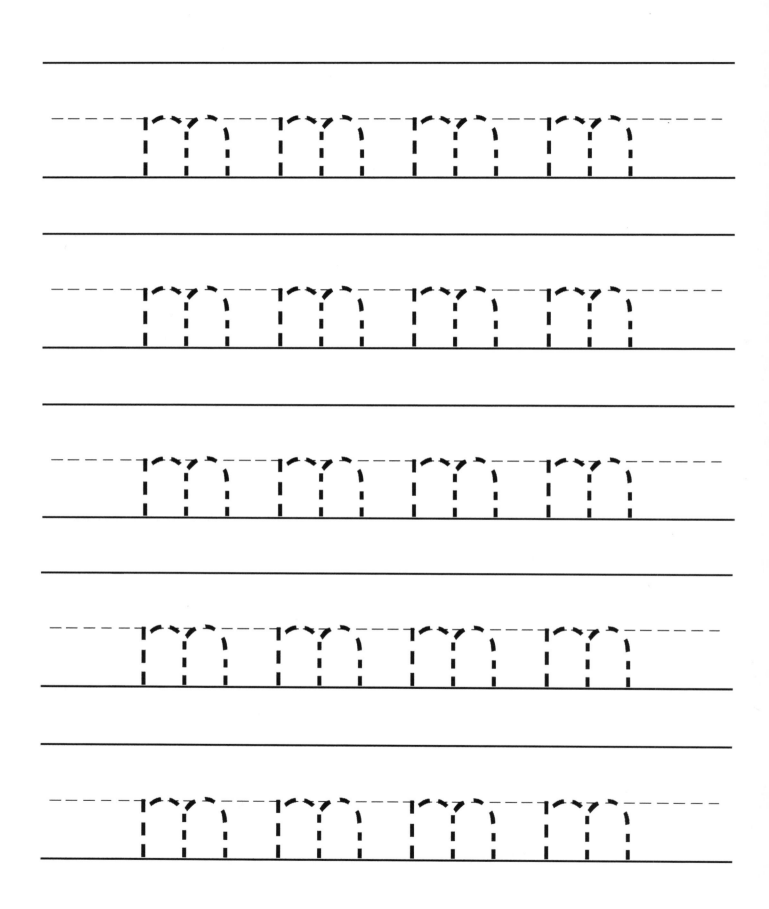

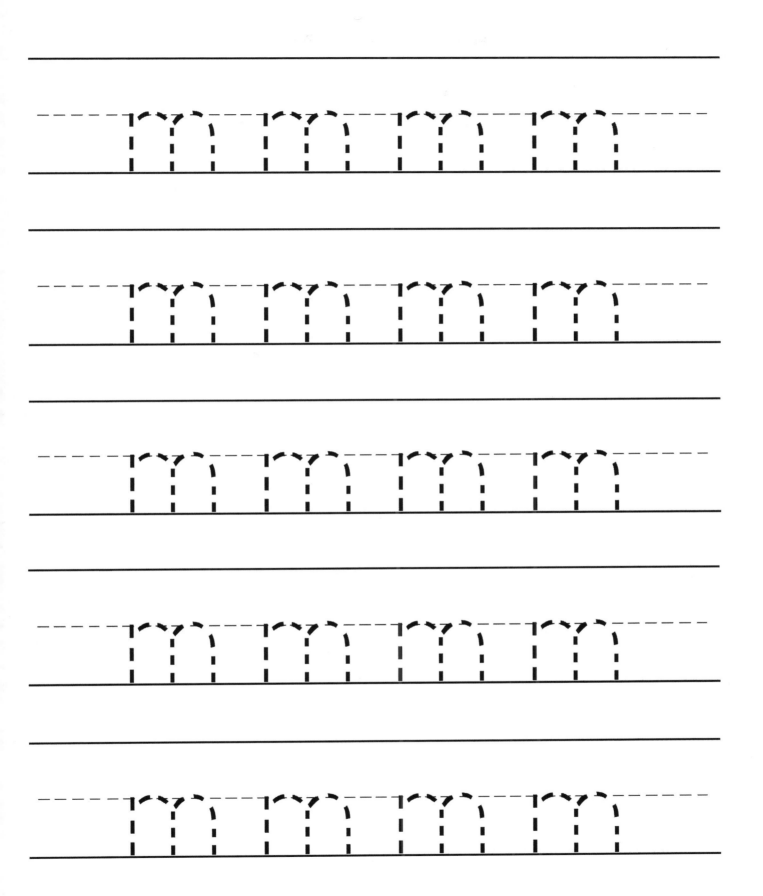

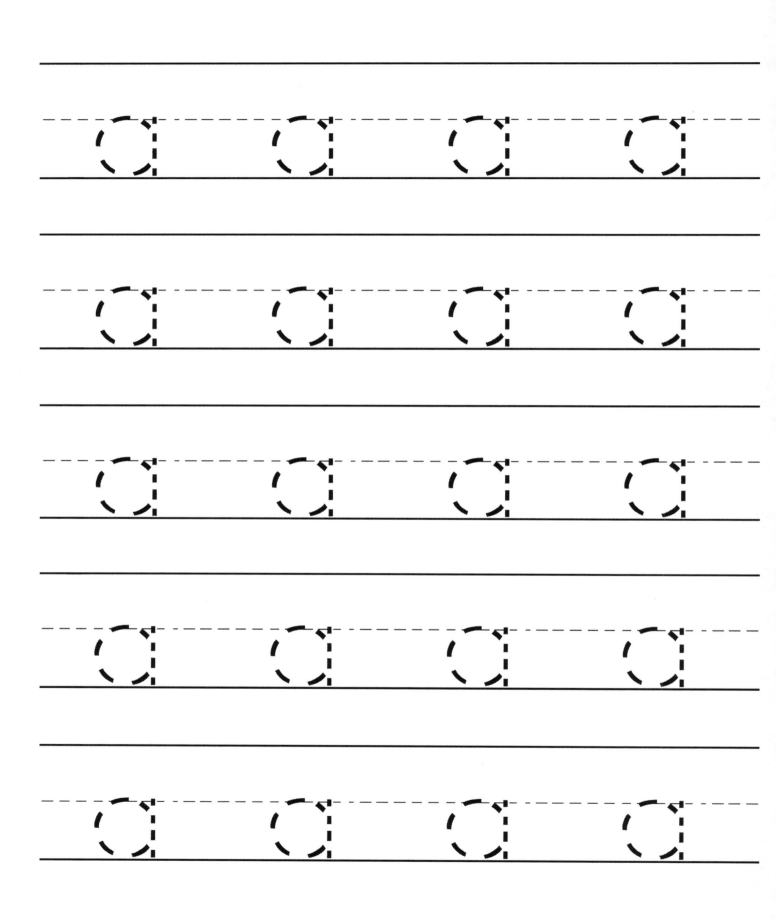

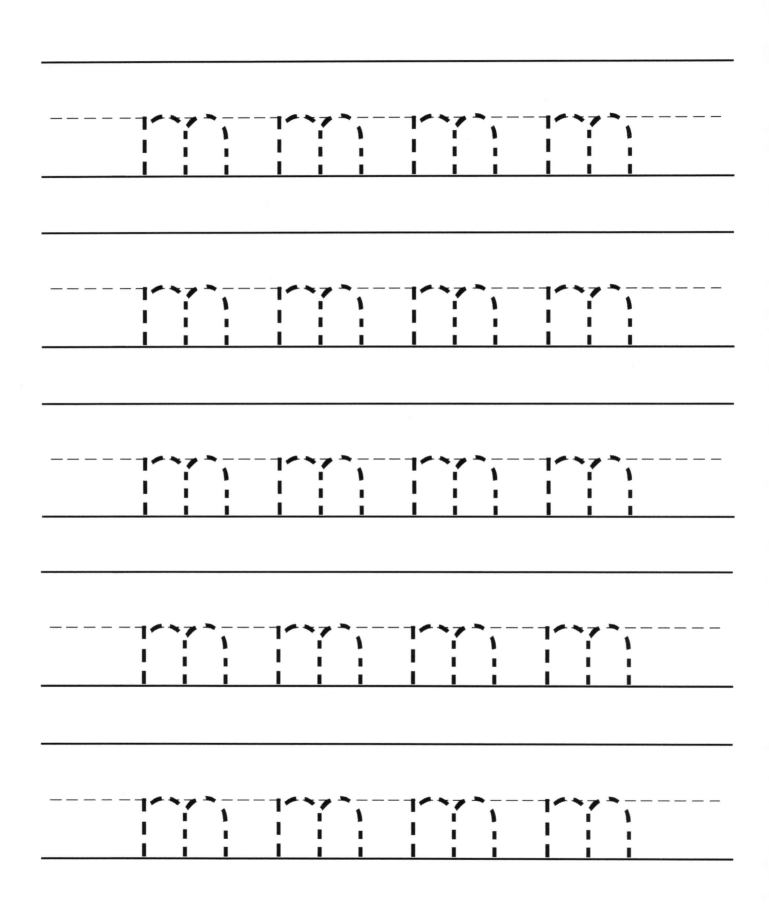

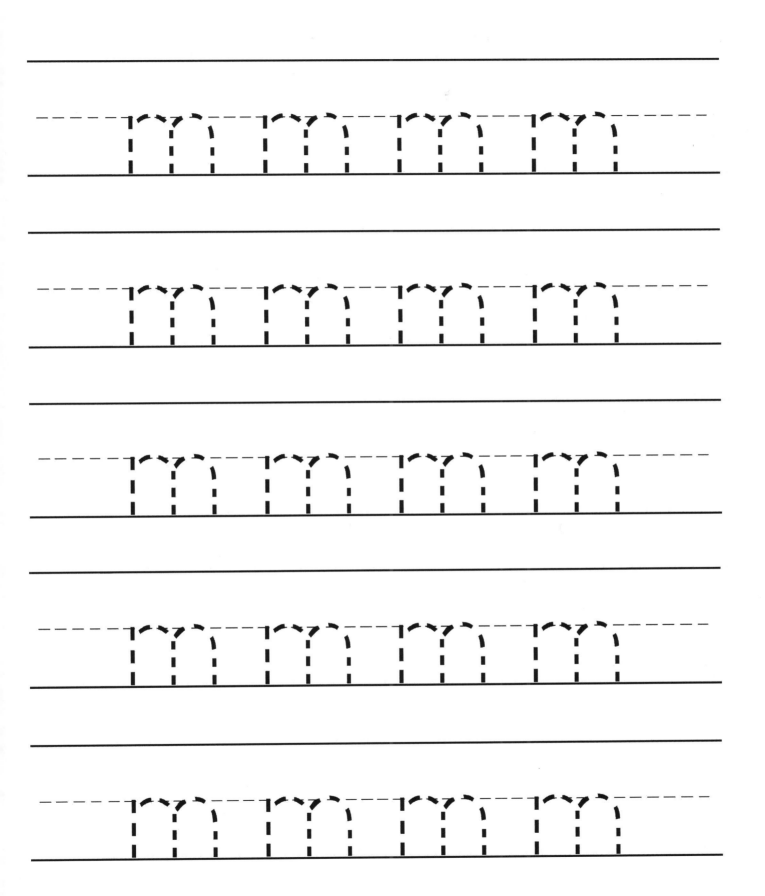

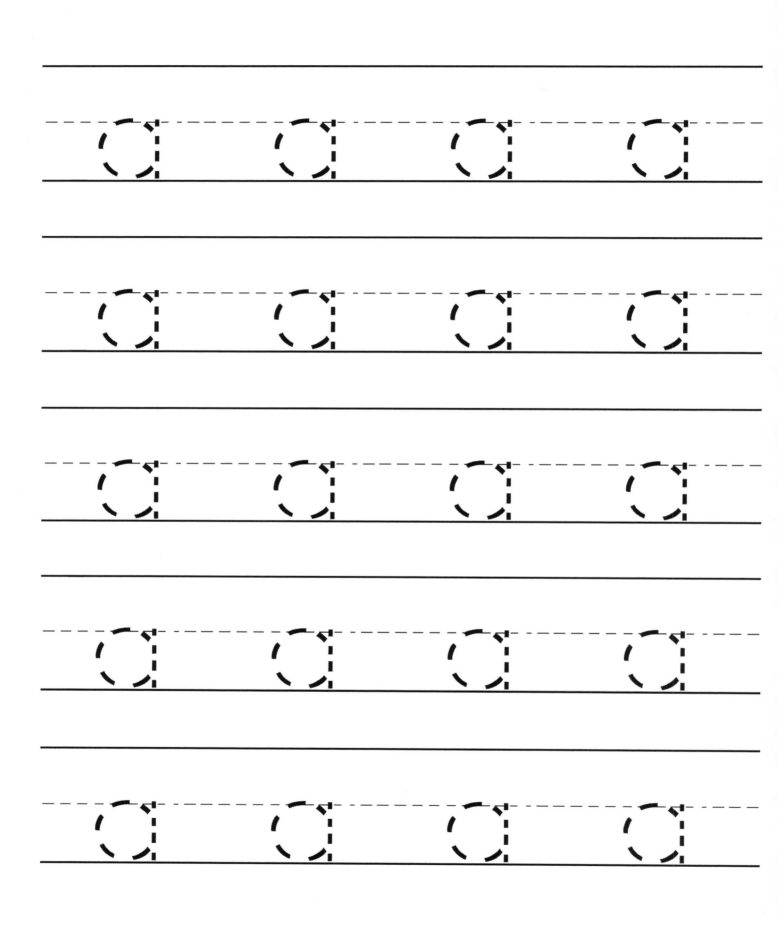

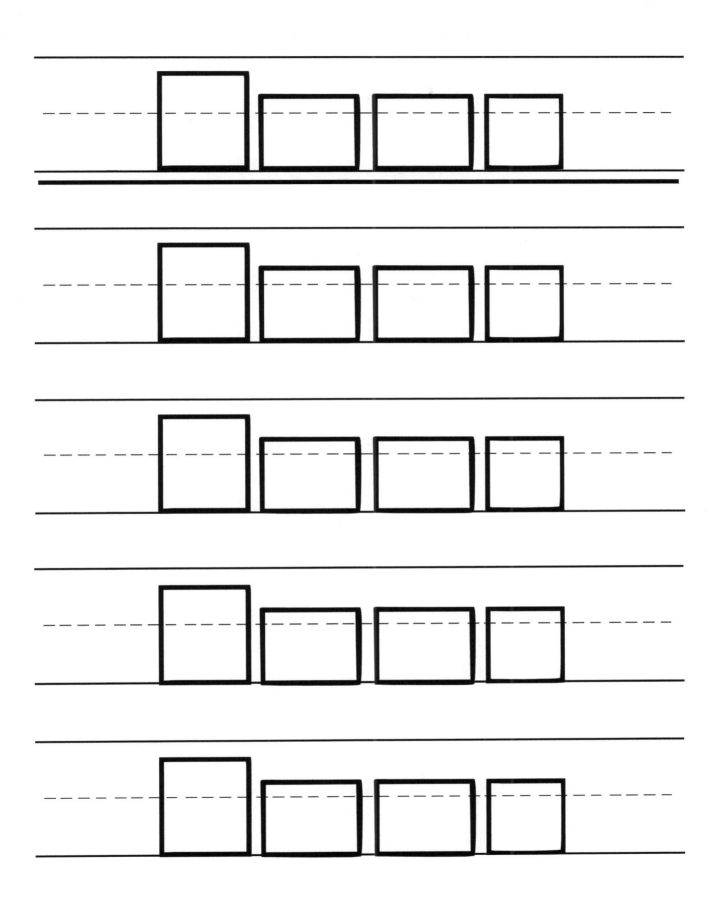

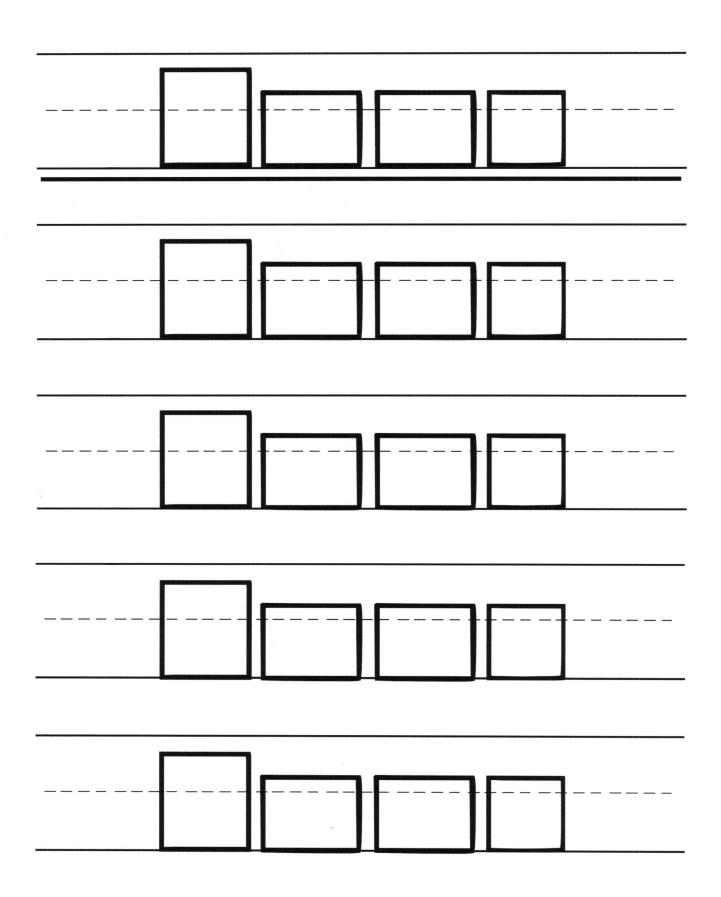

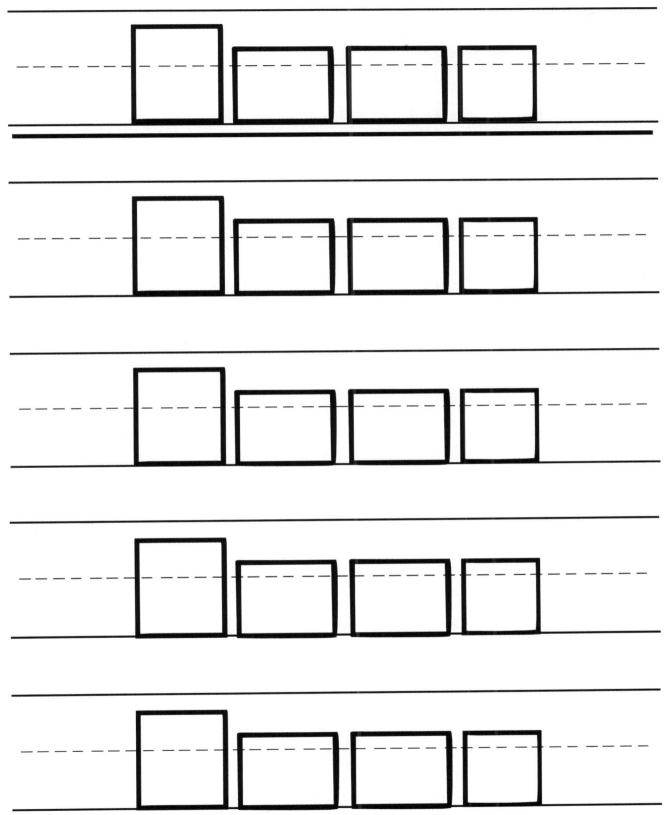

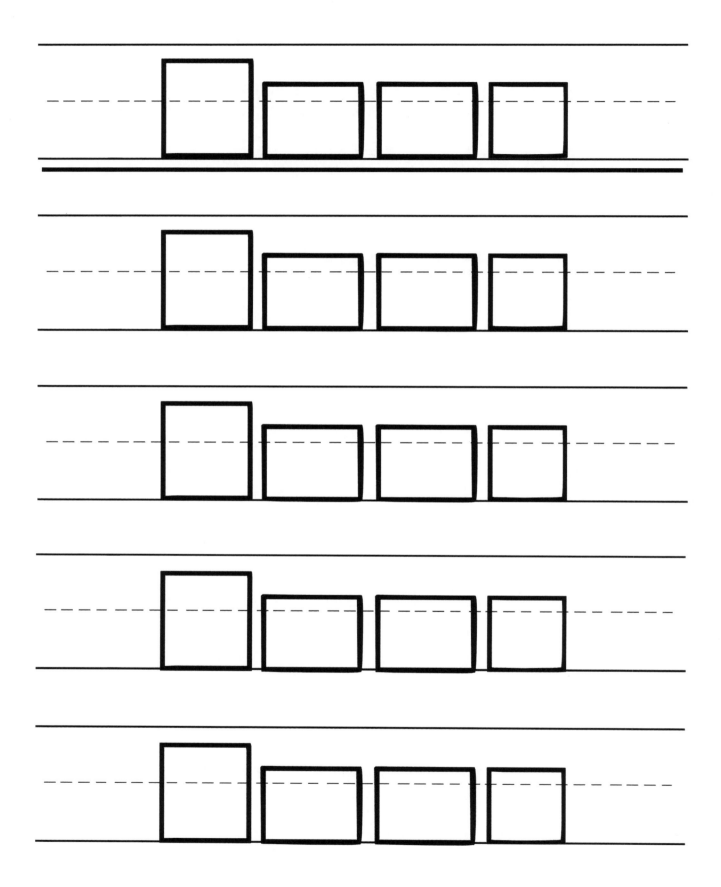

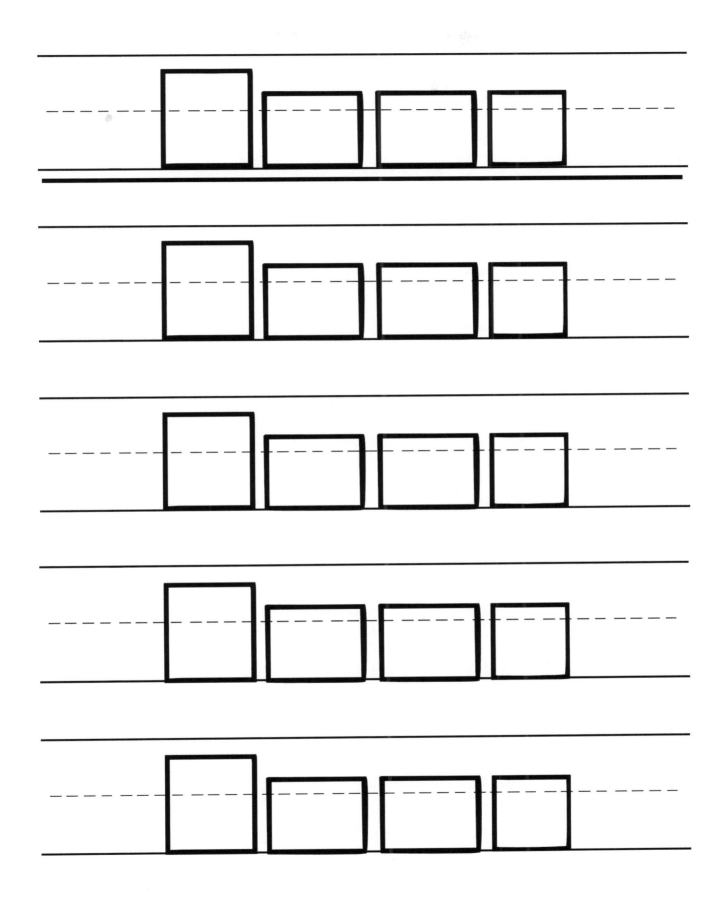

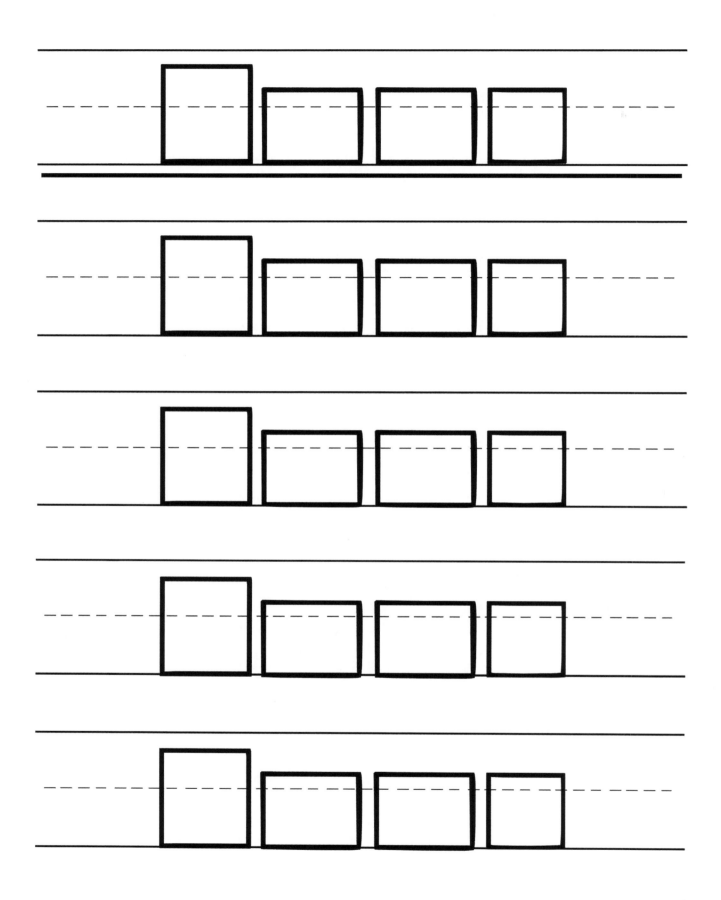

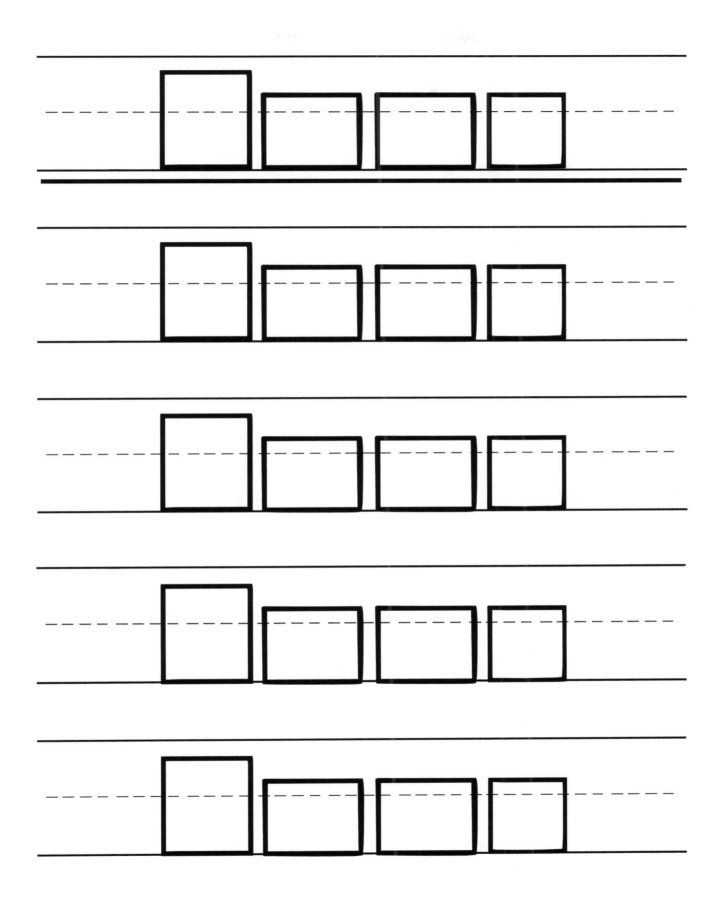

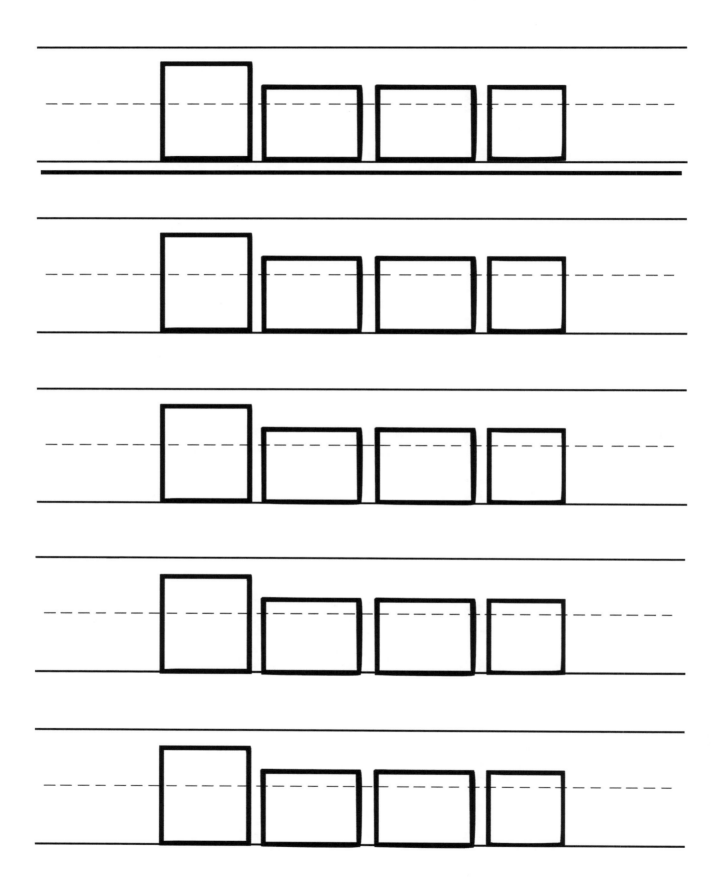

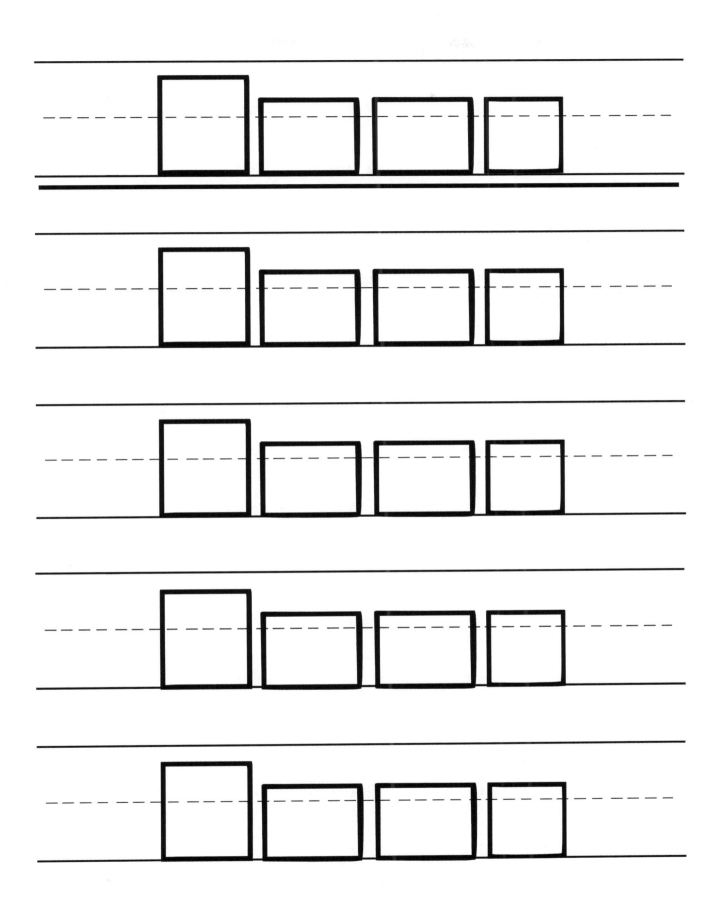

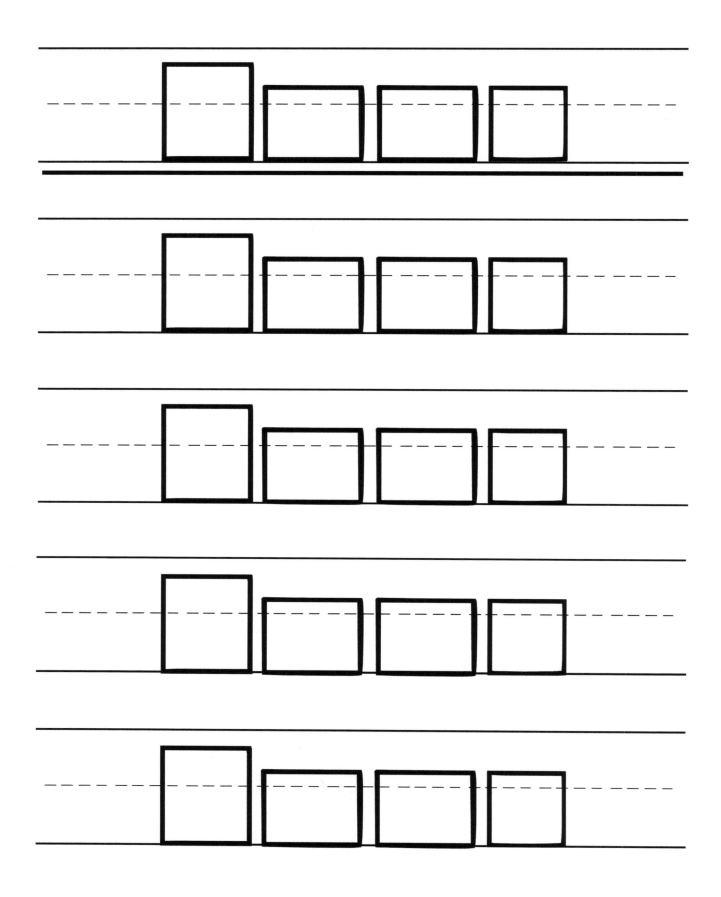

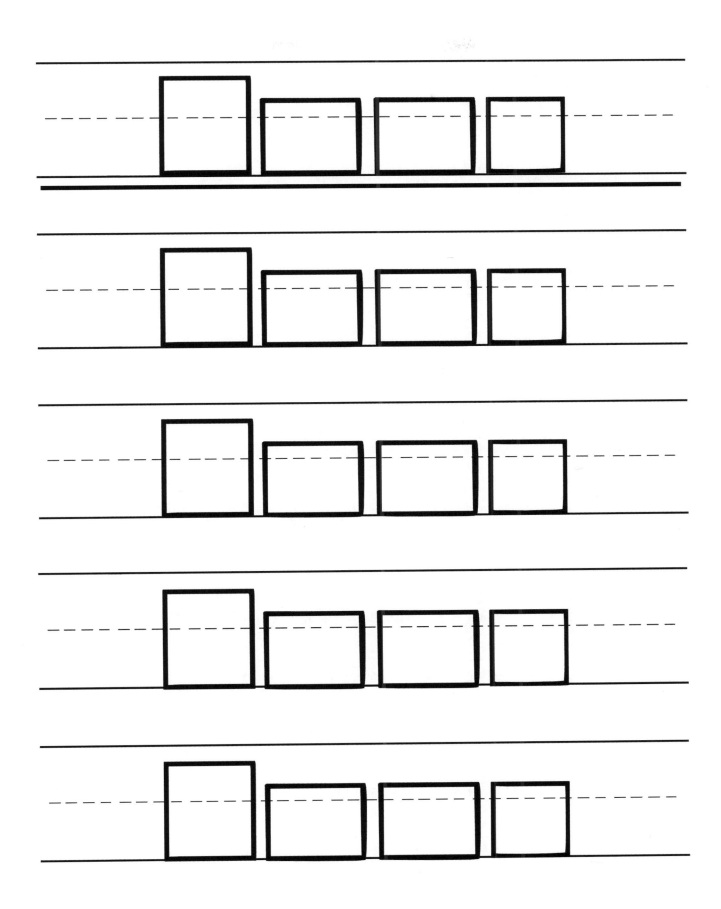

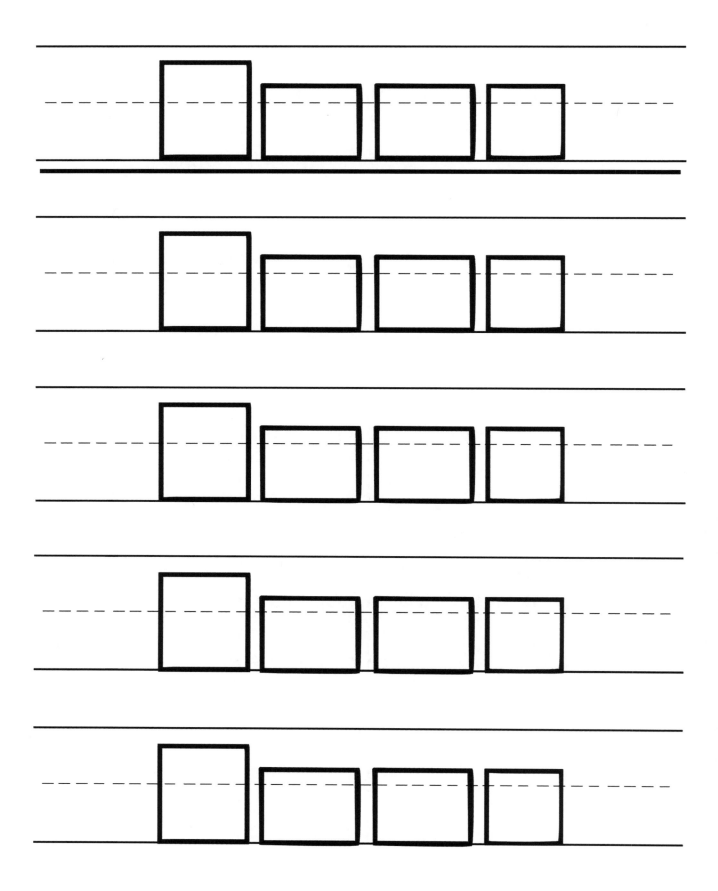

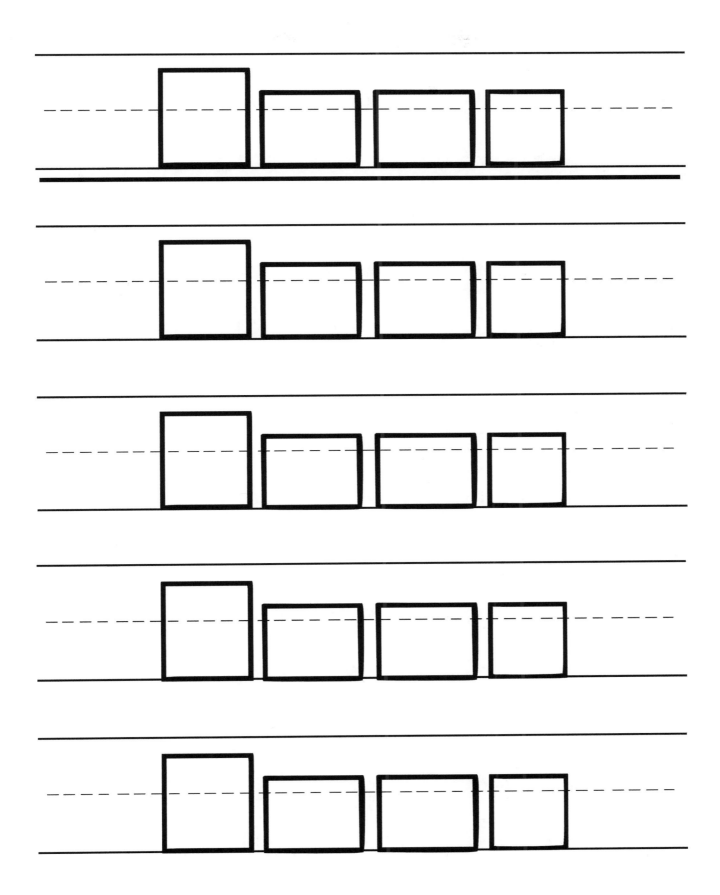

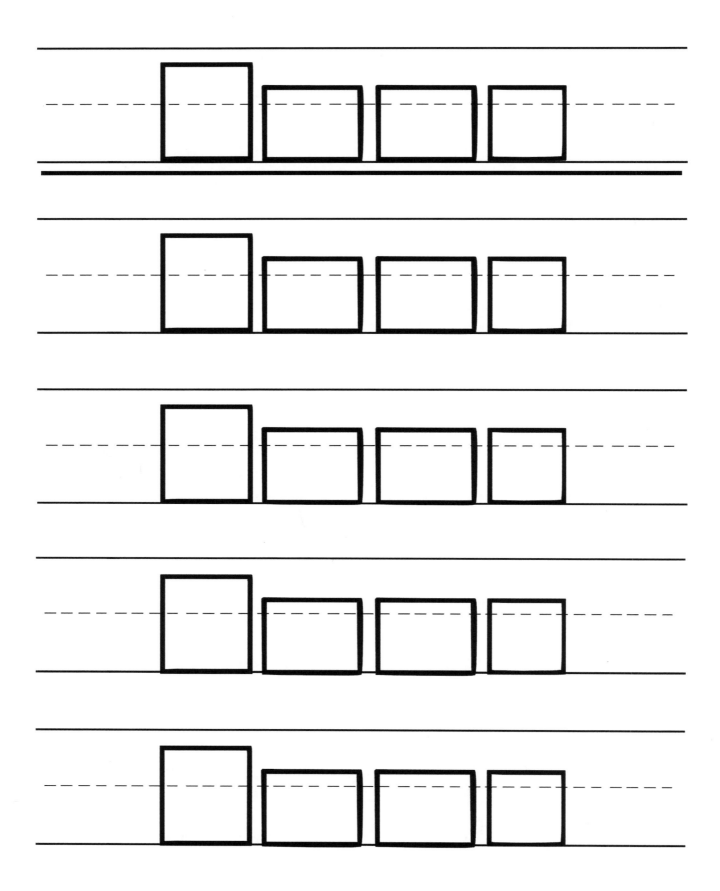

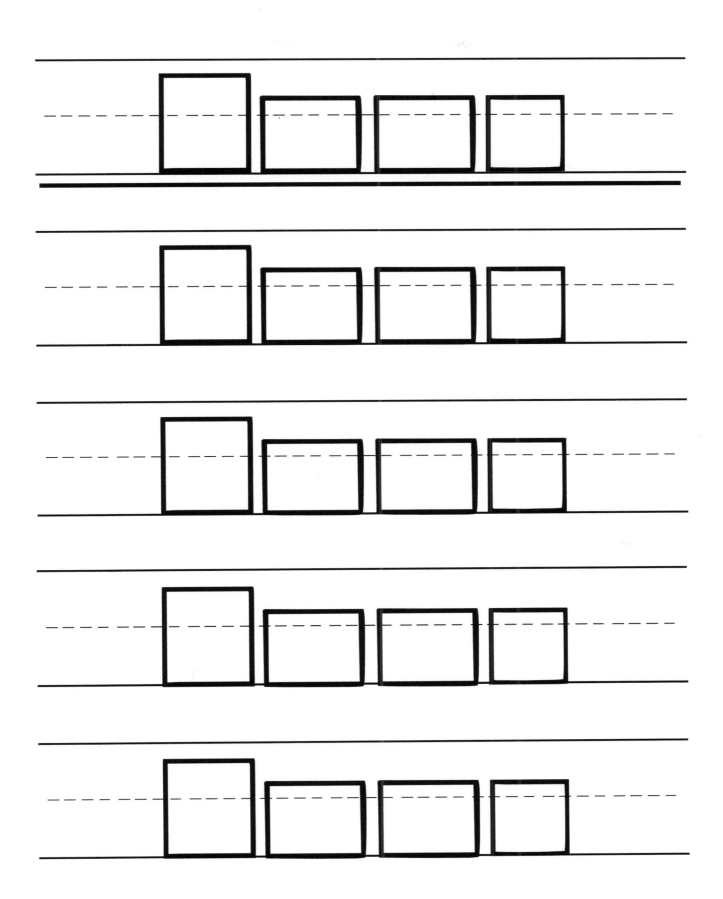

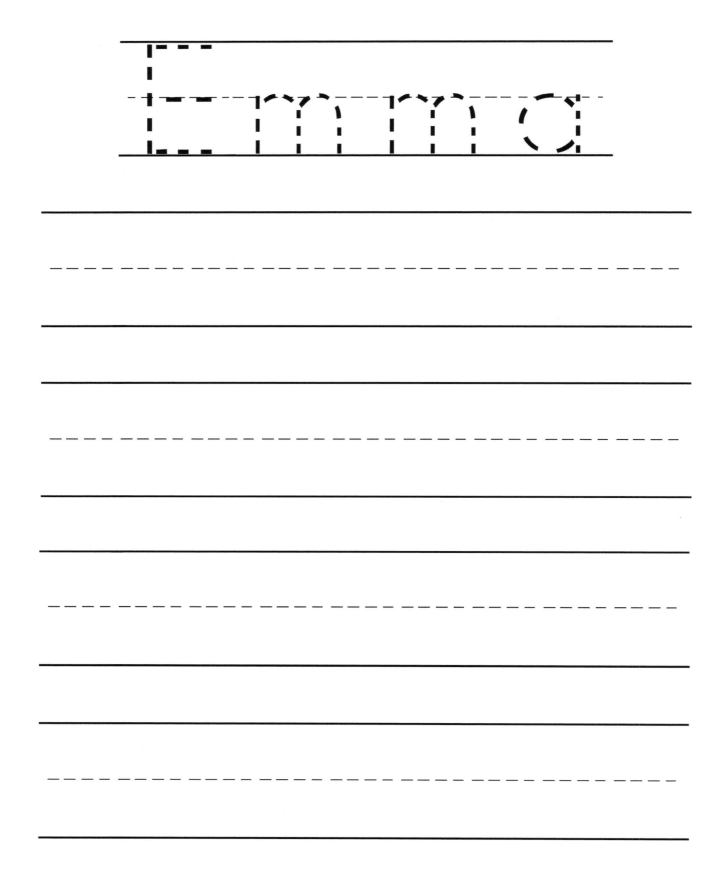

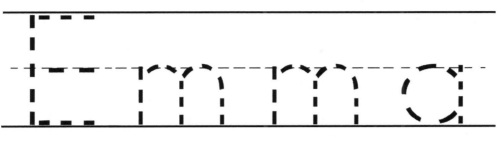

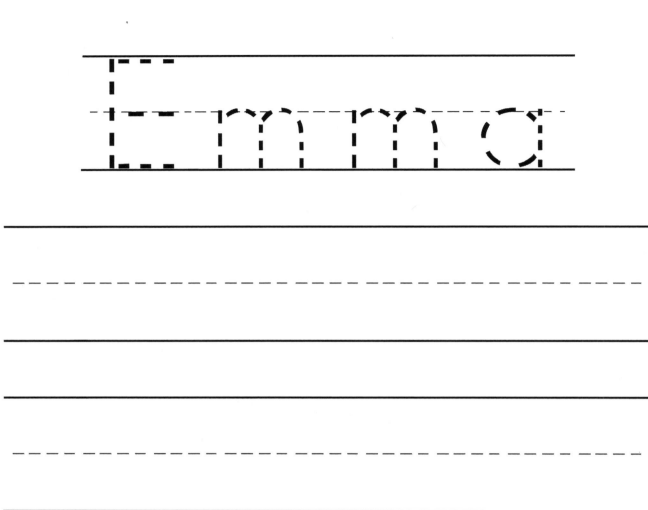

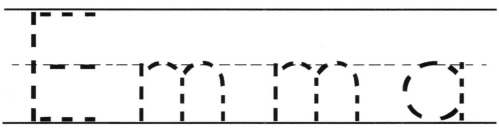

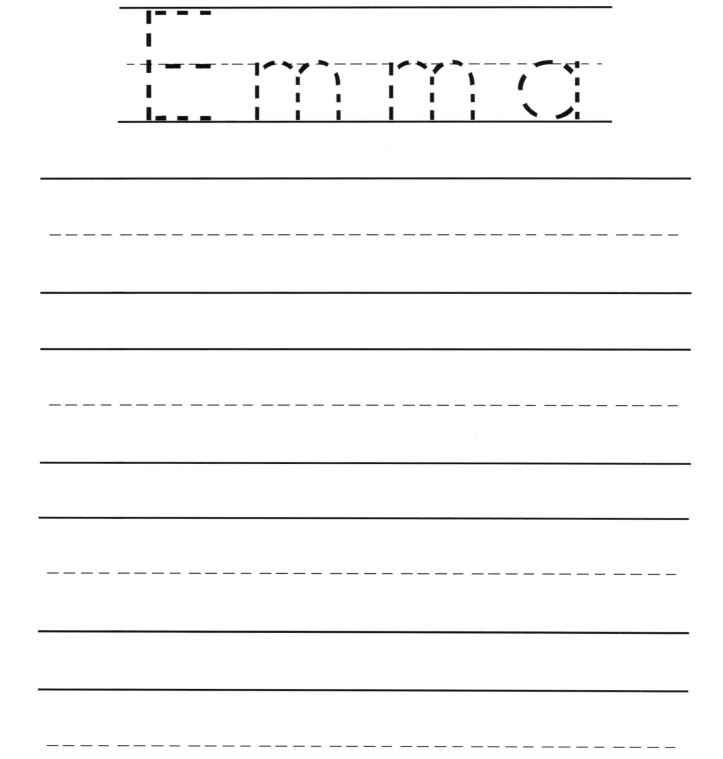

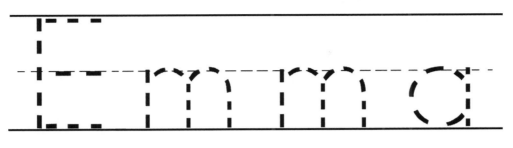

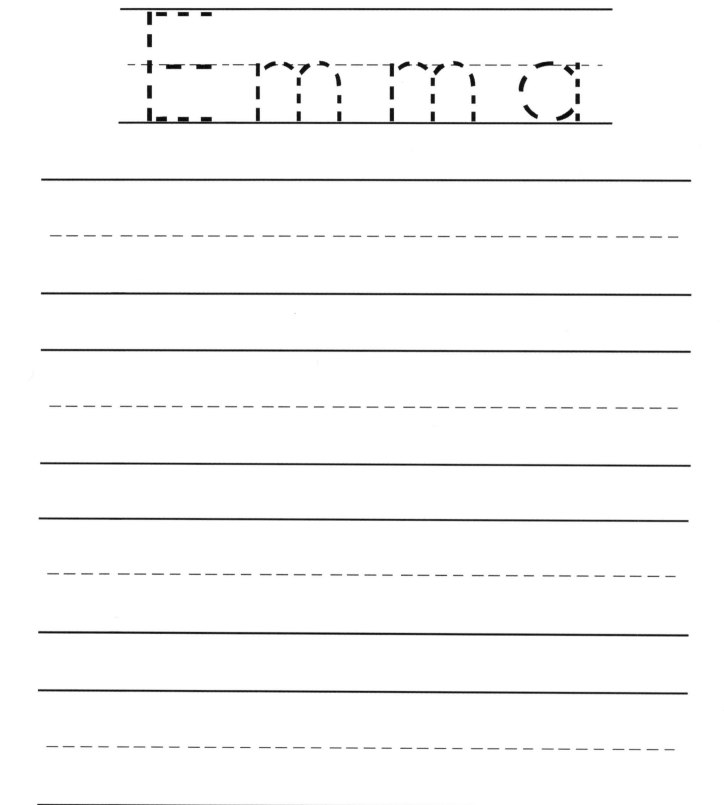

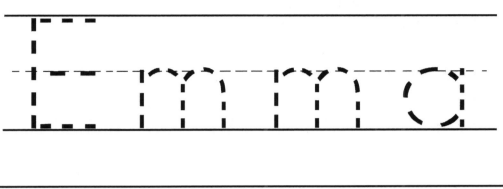

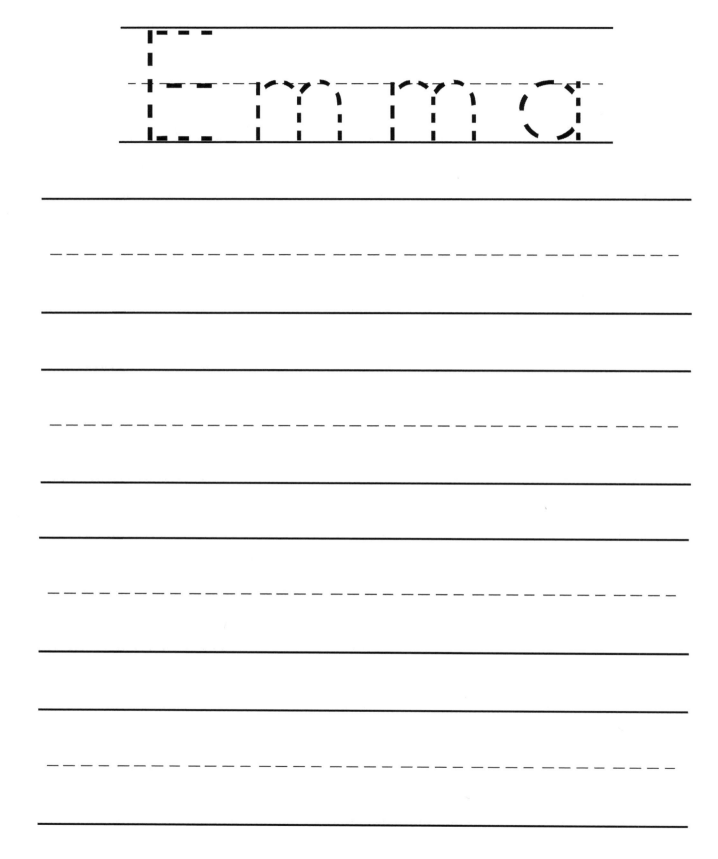

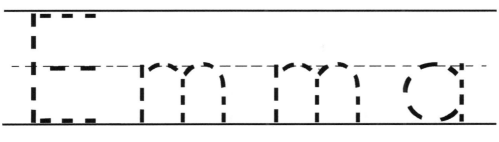

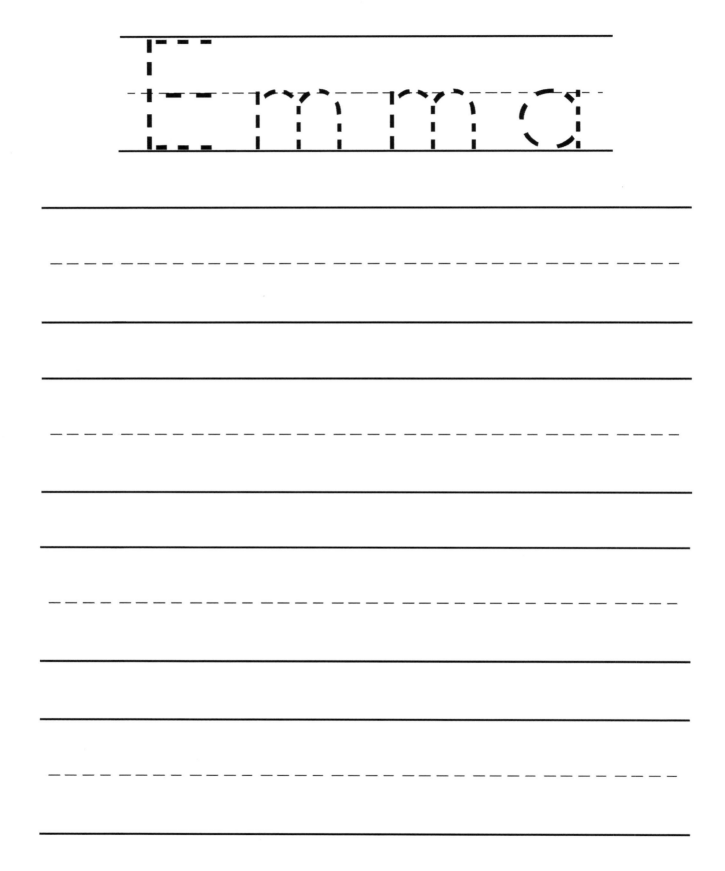

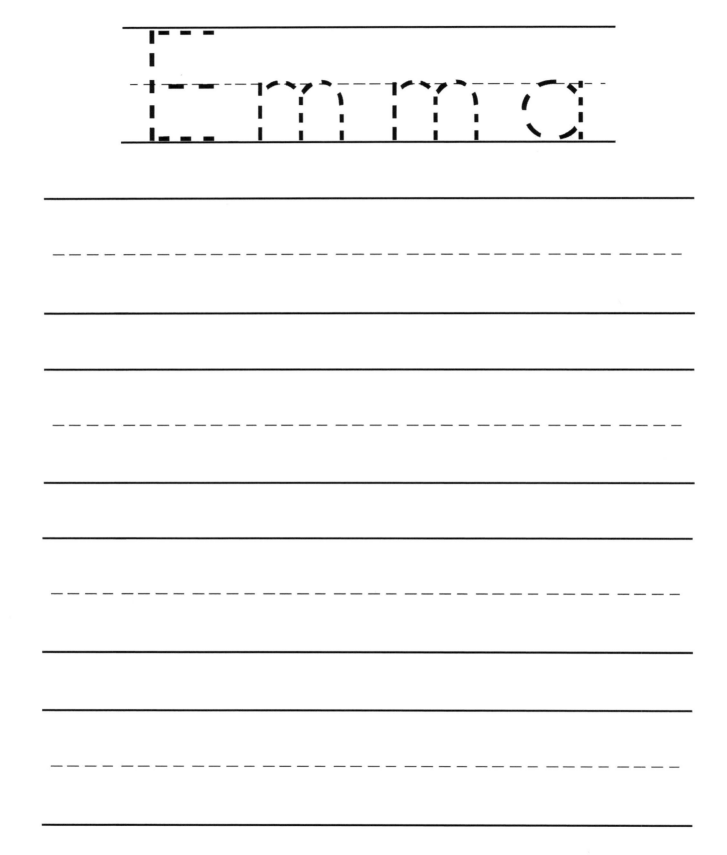

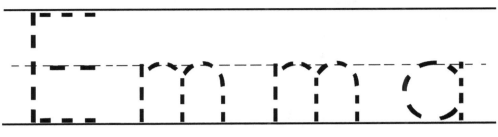

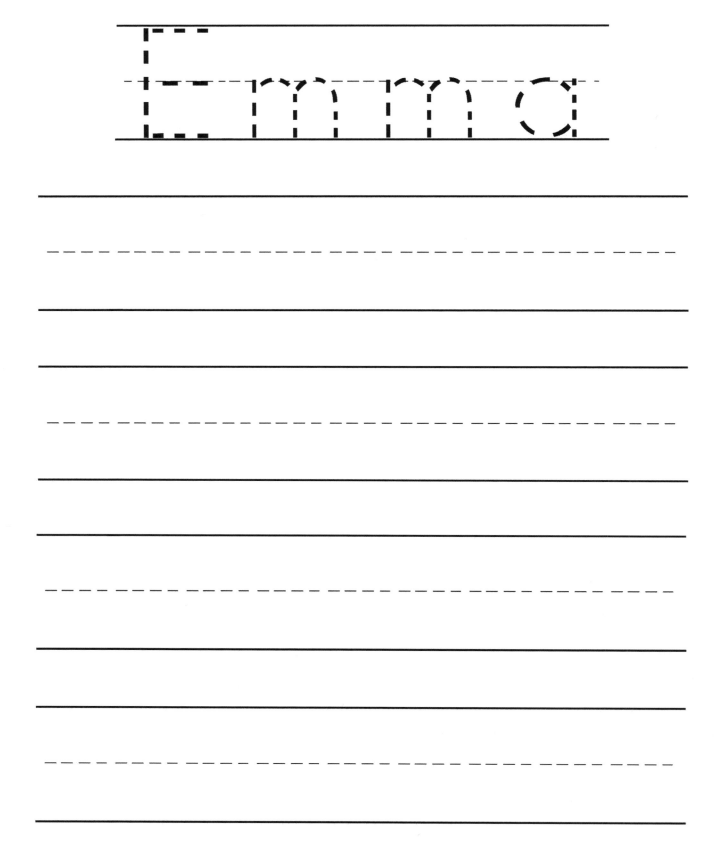

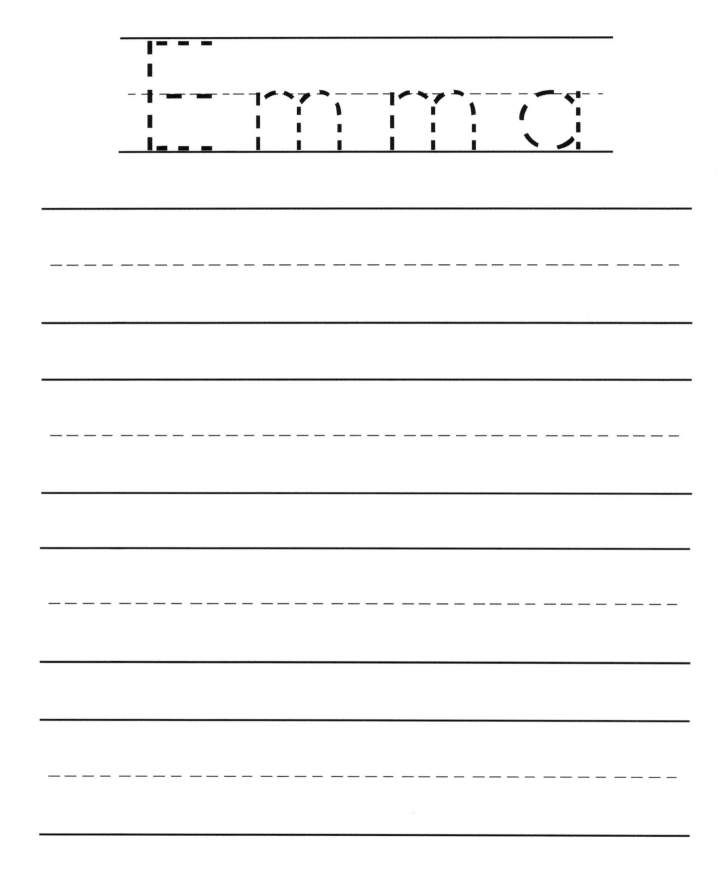

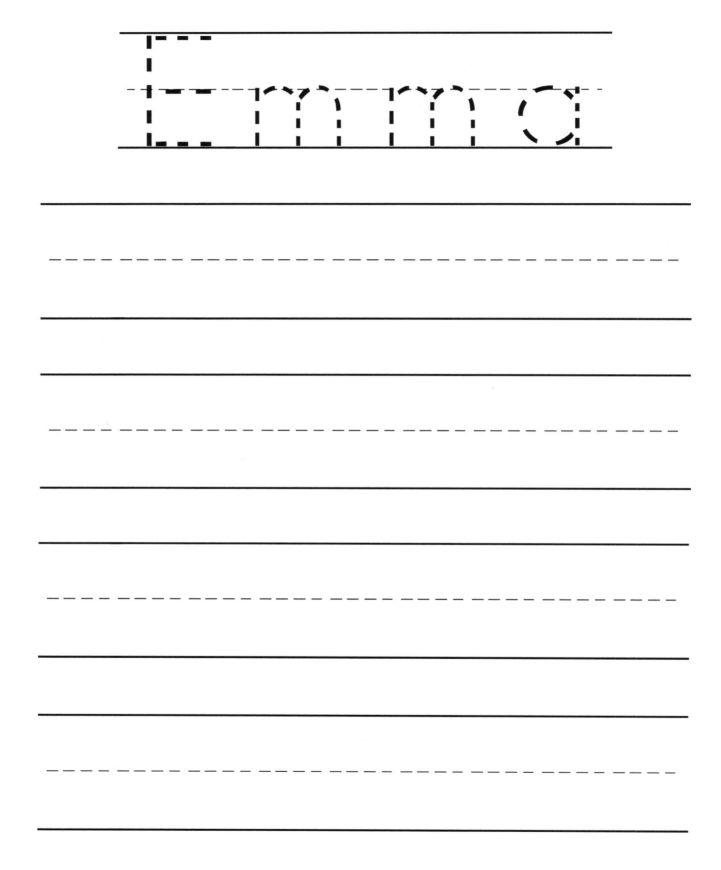

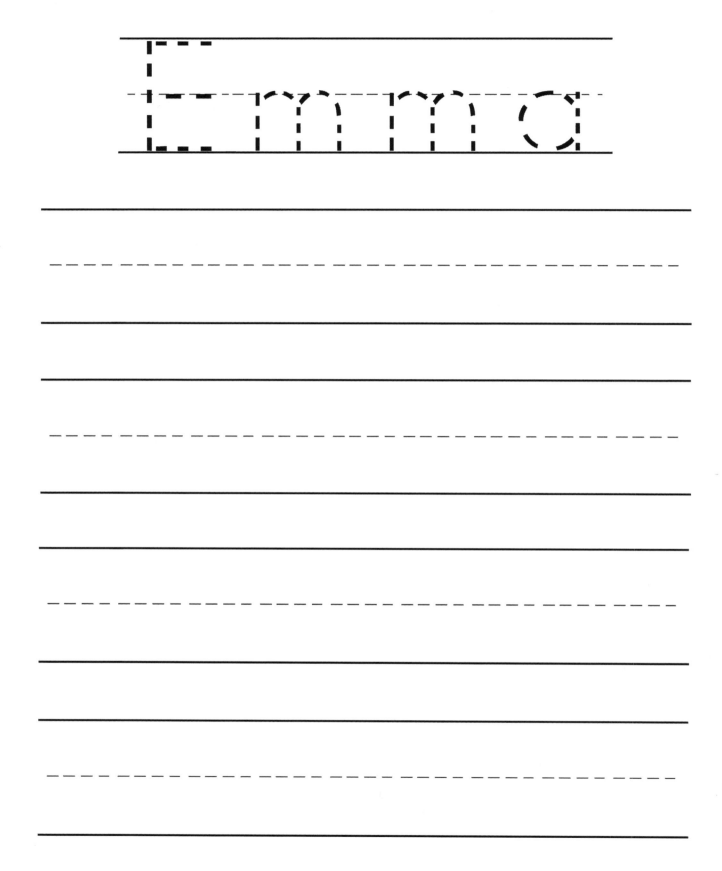

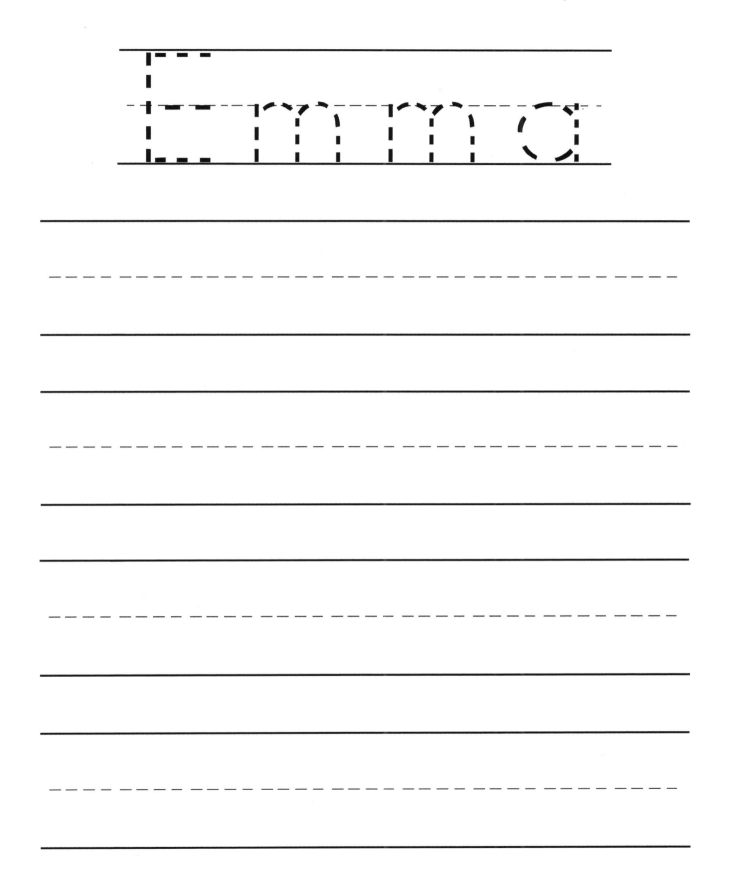

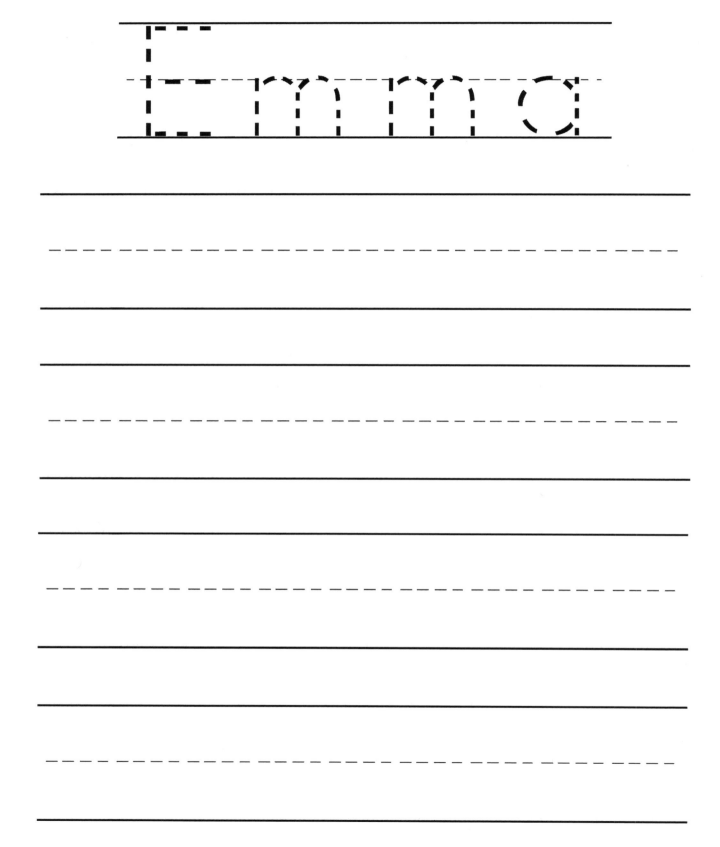

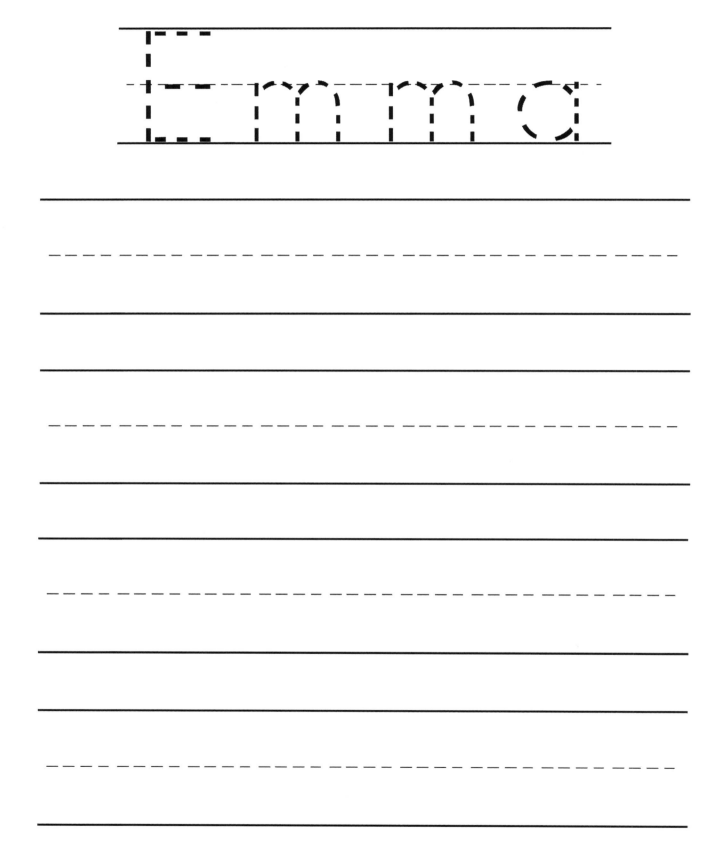

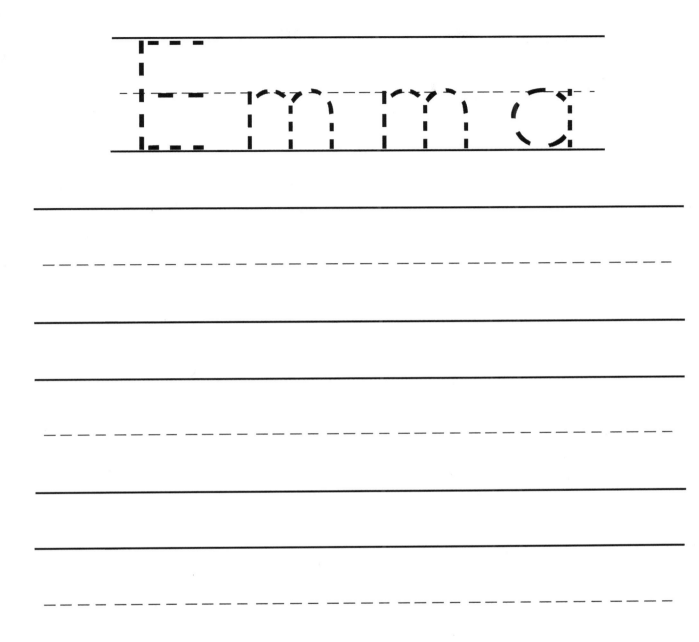

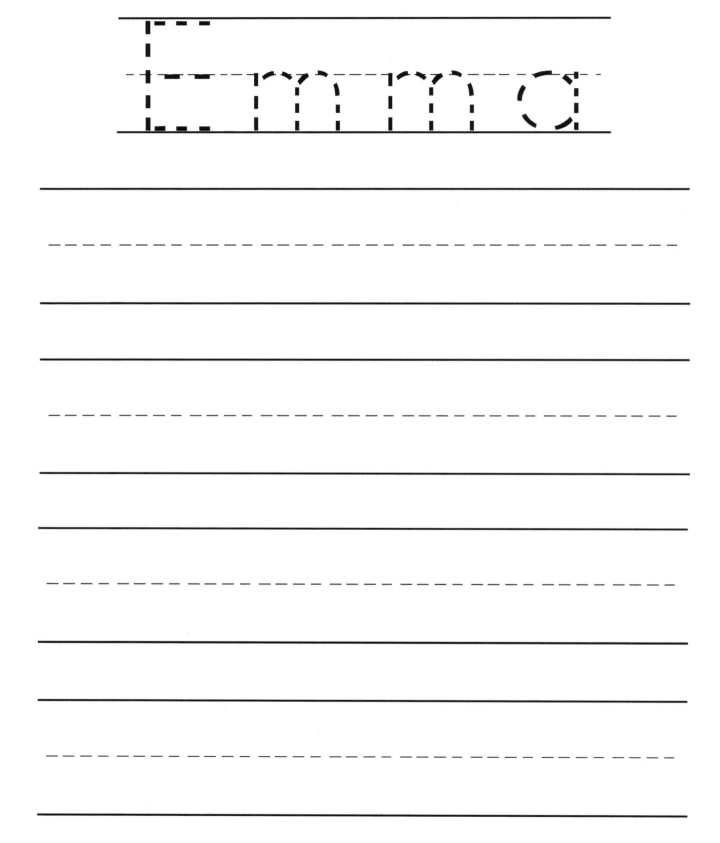

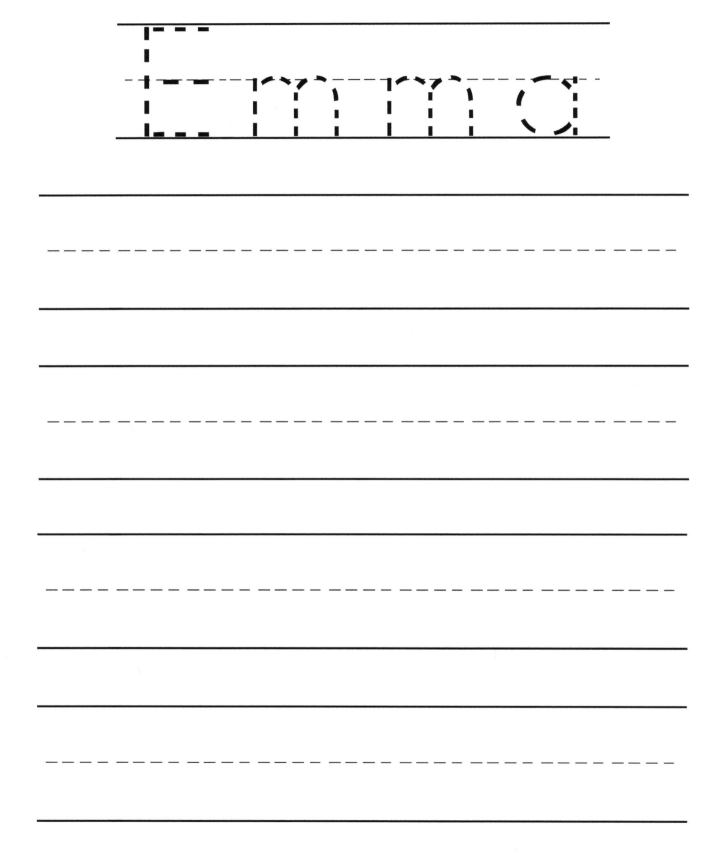

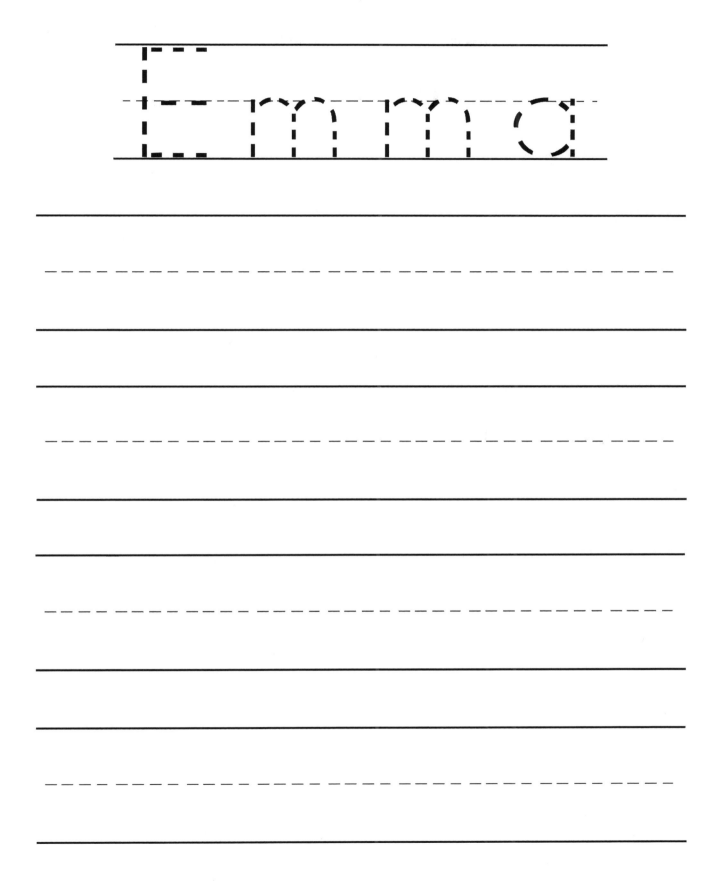

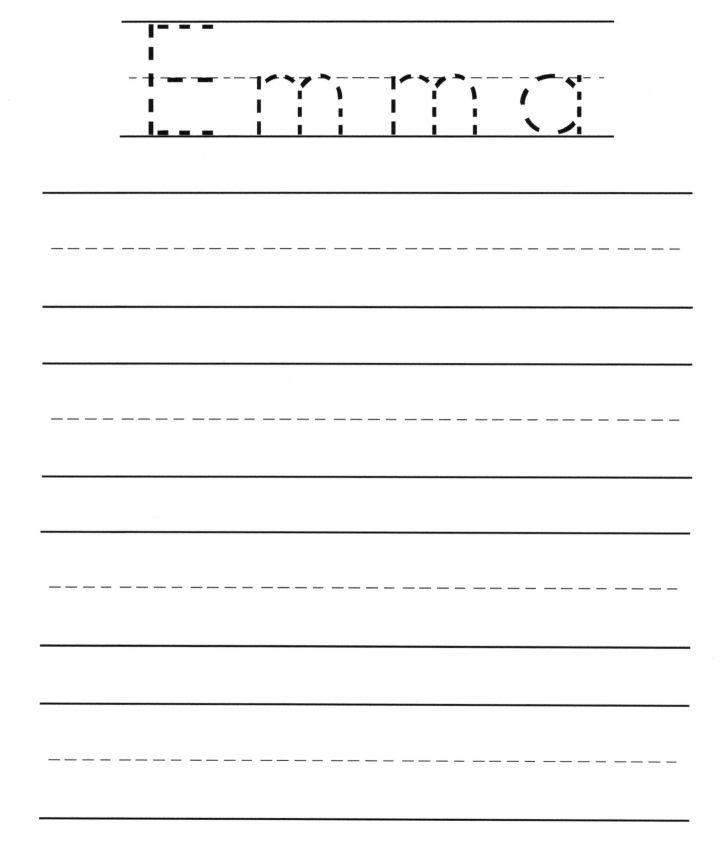

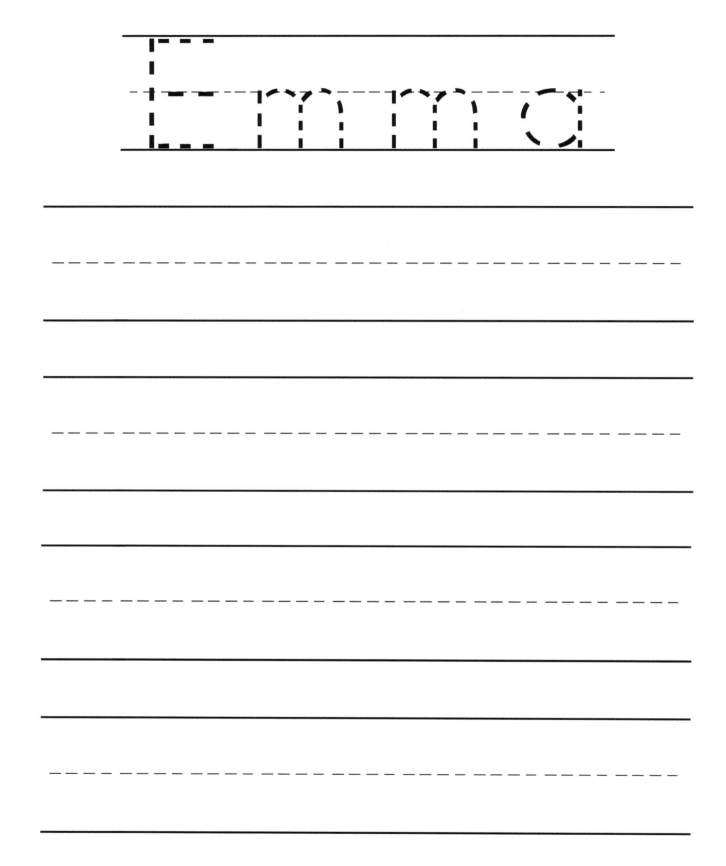

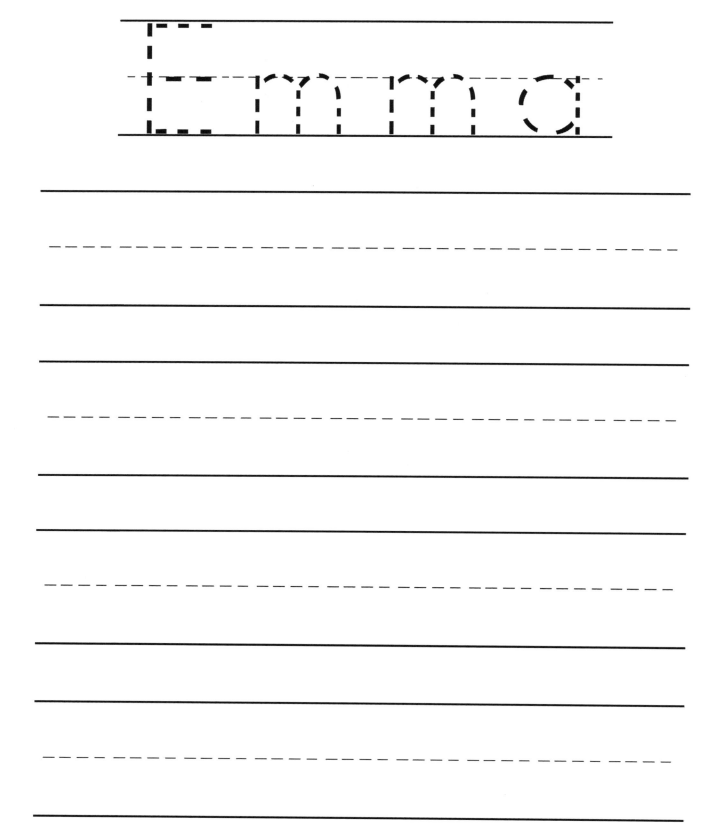

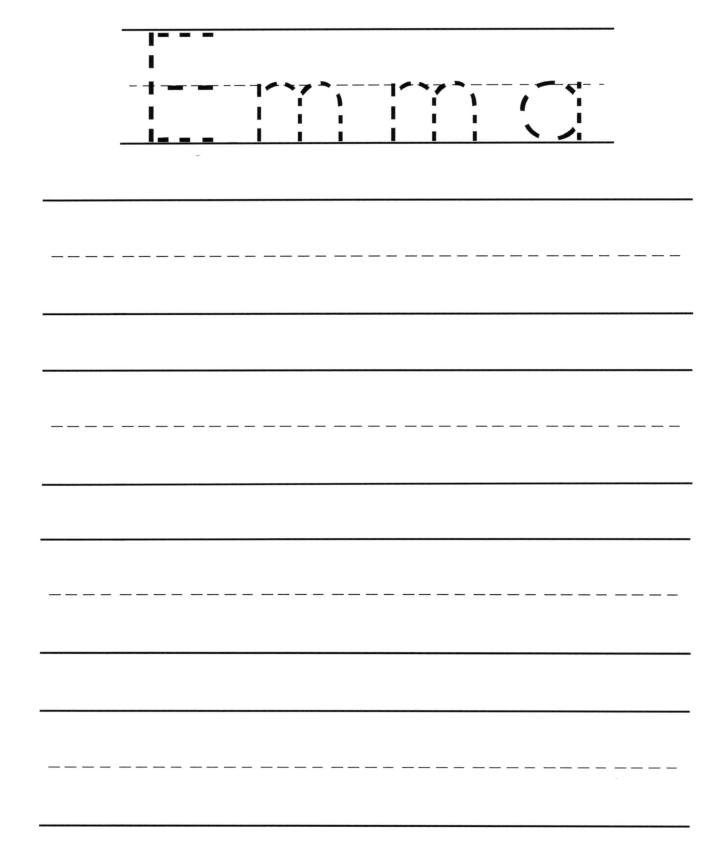

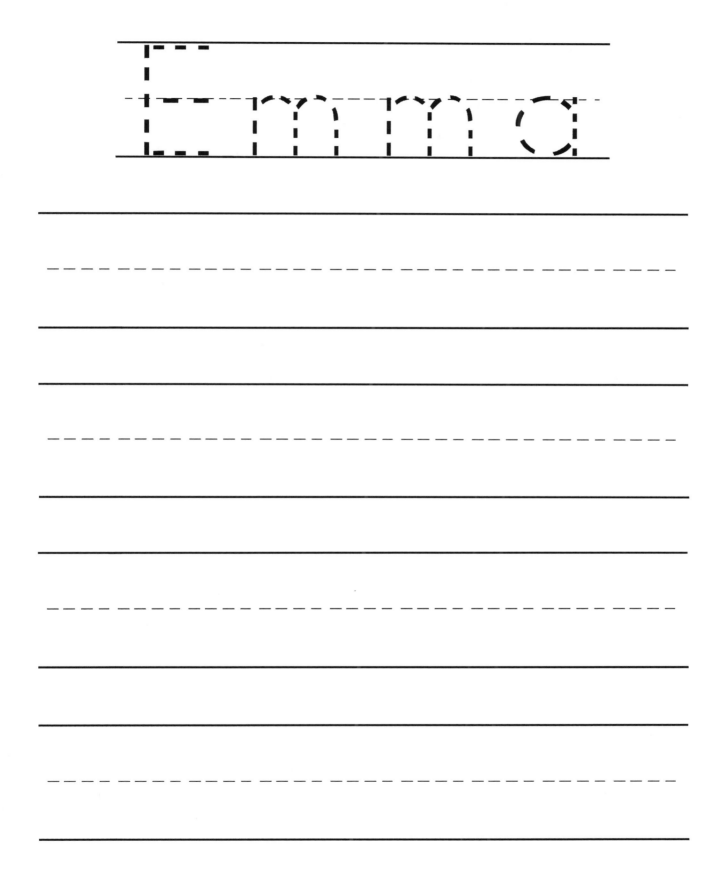

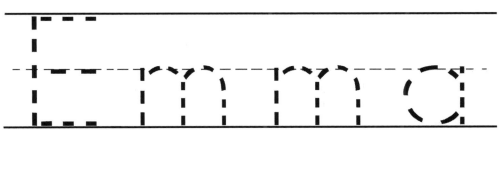

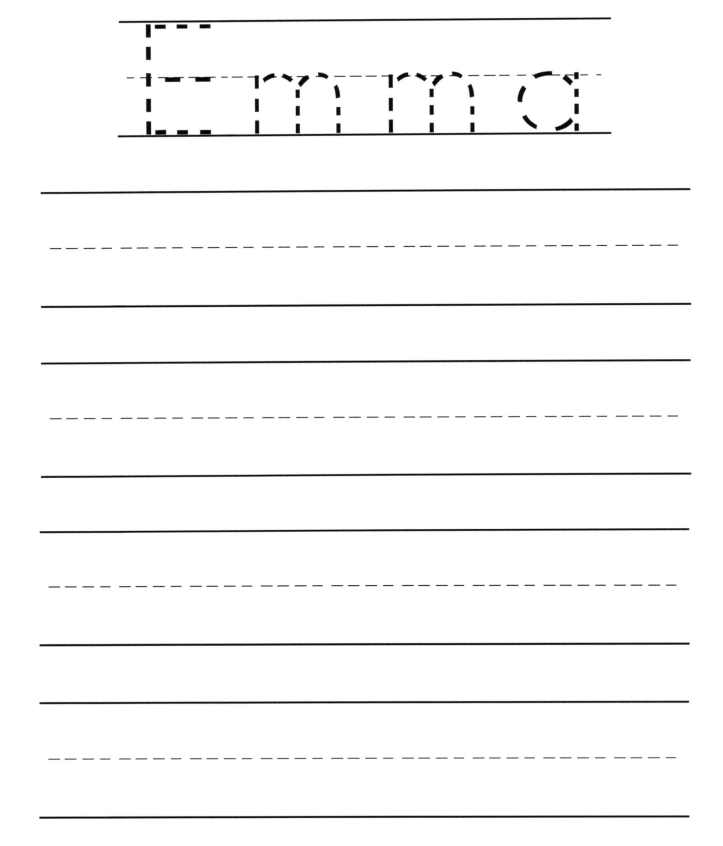